THE

ORIGIN AND GROWTH

OF

VILLAGE COMMUNITIES IN INDIA

THE ORIGIN AND GROWTH OF VILLAGE COMMUNITIES IN INDIA

BY

B. H. BADEN-POWELL, M. A., C. I. E.

GYAN

Published by

Gyan Publishing House
5, Ansari Road
Daryaganj, New Delhi-110002
Phone: 011-47034999, 9811692060
E-mail: books@gyanbooks.com

Distribution Network
gyanbooks.com
India, USA, Canada, UK, Australia, France

ISBN: 978-81-212-8230-7 (PB)
First Published, 1899

2nd Impression 2023

Printed at: Gyan Press, Delhi.

THE ORIGIN AND GROWTH OF VILLAGE COMMUNITIES IN INDIA
Author: B. H. BADEN-POWELL

THE ORIGIN AND GROWTH OF VILLAGE COMMUNITIES IN INDIA

THE
ORIGIN AND GROWTH
OF
VILLAGE COMMUNITIES IN INDIA

BY

B. H. BADEN-POWELL, M.A., C.I.E.

LONDON
SWAN SONNENSCHEIN & CO., LIM.
NEW YORK: CHARLES SCRIBNER'S SONS
1899

PREFACE

It cannot be necessary to write a formal preface to so small a book. But I may be allowed to make use of the space for two purposes. First, I have to express my thanks to Prof. W. J. Ashley, M.A., of Harvard University, and late Fellow of Lincoln College, Oxford, not only for the suggestion that a short account of the Indian village should be written, but for valuable advice and criticism in the course of writing it.

Secondly, I have to say a few words about the (not very frequent) Indian words (Hindi, Persian, etc.) which occur. I have avoided them wherever I could; but sometimes they are needed for the sake of readers in India, or because there is no satisfactory equivalent; partly also because they show that the thing indicated is, or is not, indigenous; that it has been borrowed from the Moslems, or is an older Hindu institution. Now, the only tolerable way in which such words can be given in print, is by transliterating into Roman character; and people then say "we do not know how they should be pronounced."

But for practical purposes, it is quite easy to pronounce Indian words at least intelligibly. Only remember that they are *not English*, and in particular, that the letter "a" (without accent) which so commonly occurs must *never* be pronounced with the peculiar sound of the English "flat," "that," "many," etc. It is *uniformly* like the *u* in "bun," so that the Hindi syllables *mani*, *e.g.*, are read like the English word "money." Each vowel has a short or unaccented use, also a broad or accented, thus :—

a—*â* (as in English) "bun"—"ba(r)n"
i—*î* " " "pit"—"peat"
u—*û* " " "pull"—"pool"

(*ê*) is regarded as a diphthong, and is always with "ay" (*têl* = "tale"), *ô* is always long as in "post."

These sounds are invariable. I have not marked the variations in the consonants, except to write *q* when the Arabic (k) is indicated. But it will be well to state the *th* is *never* sibilant (as in "this" or "thin") in Indian dialects, it is only *t* with an aspirate; *g* is always hard, *never* as in "gin" (which would be *j*).

OXFORD, *July*, 1899. B. H. B-P.

CONTENTS

INDIAN VILLAGE COMMUNITIES

I

GENERAL HISTORY OF THE QUESTION OF INDIAN VILLAGE ORIGINS

THE object of this little book is to explain, in the compass of a few pages, and as untechnically as possible, the nature and origin of Indian village communities, with special reference to the commonly received theories about them. Many people have heard vaguely that the villages represent an ancient "communal" holding of land; others have heard that this theory has been much doubted. They would perhaps like to know more about the subject without having to make a prolonged or very detailed study

These Indian communities are living, and not, like the "Teutonic mark," dead. The importance of observing and understanding them for the purposes of the comparative history of institutions, and for economic science in general, is admitted on all hands. But often as "the village" is alluded to in histories or other books on Indian subjects, it is dealt with chiefly as the creature of theory—a thing in the air, rather than an existing institution, which can be studied with reference to historic facts, times, and places, and to tribes and families of known race and location. And the year 1870 (or some nearly approaching period) may be taken as the birth-time (in England) of a general theory regarding the origin and nature of Indian villages. This theory obtained such wide currency that it soon seemed to be beyond the reach of question. All Indian villages were regarded as having been originally constituted in a single (typical) form; this form being, consequently, spoken of as archaic date and of "Aryan" parentage. So conceived, "the village community" was asserted to represent a group of persons or households who cultivated and owned their land "in common"; it was, in short, an important and widespread oriental survival of that "ownership in common" which was believed to have been universally antecedent to the development of individual property in later times. The best known exposition of this theory is to be found in the works of the late Sir H. S. Maine, especially in his "Village Communities of the East and West,"[1] and in several lectures, afterwards collected

[1] The first edition is dated 1871. My quotations are from the third edition, and indicated by the letters "V. C."

in a book entitled "The Early History of Institutions."[1] Let us, however, not misunderstand the author's position in these works. He treats the conception of "the village" as if it were based on a certainty. The evidence he possessed established so much, at least, that they were joint-bodies or close, self-managing communities. That was enough. He never proposed to go into detail, or give a complete account of their origin or history. The village is conceived in the abstract, and is introduced as a well-known phenomenon. It is the extreme generality of his view, expressed, as it is, in lucid phrases, that caused it to be so easily and so widely read and remembered.

About ten years after the publication of these works, it fell to my lot (under circumstances which need not be detailed) to prepare an account of the Land Systems and Land-Revenue Administration of British India. This was first published in Calcutta. And ten years later a new and more complete work on the same subject was prepared and published at Oxford.[2] At this time the village theory was in full possession of the field, and was supported by all the authority of Sir H. S. Maine's name, as well as recommended by the charm of his style and the suggestiveness of his method. It is true that, as far as concerns the general

[1] Dated 1874-5; indicated as "E. H. I."

[2] "The Land Systems of British India," 3 vols. : Clarendon Press, 1892. In the sequel this is referred to as "L. S. B. I."

prevalence of primitive communal ownership and the "Teutonic mark," the works of M. Fustel de Coulanges and others had already raised serious doubts; but their argument hardly touched the Indian phenomena—at least directly. However that may be, all this time the materials for a detailed study of the Indian villages in all parts of the great empire had been rapidly accumulating. Evidence, far superior in character to anything that had before been obtained, was now in print; and it covered a much wider field of inquiry, including provinces about which little or no information was available before 1870. Administrative Systems in India, and the Land Revenue System more especially, cannot be dealt with without giving an account of the land tenures. And to describe the *village* tenures according to the facts as they appeared in the light of the fuller evidence, was to make something of a new departure. It was not, indeed, necessary, in describing the Land Revenue System, to discuss the origin of villages, or dispute theories; but even the limited account that was indispensable could not fail to suggest a widely different view of the subject. In order, therefore, to examine still further the facts in the light of later information, it was desirable to collect the available evidence in a separate book.[1] Of this I will say no more than that it cannot be easy reading, because so

[1] "The Indian Village Community," 1 vol.: Longmans, 1896. This is referred to shortly in the sequel as "Ind. Vill. Com."

much detail is necessary, and because it is so very difficult to marshal the matter in such an order that it shall be intelligible to those who have not any long Indian experience. I find, in fact, that my meaning has often been misapprehended. It seems, therefore, desirable that an opportunity should be taken of offering (in as brief a compass as the nature of the subject will admit) a general re-statement of the case and of the general conclusions which appear to be justifiable. In doing this, it is necessary to indicate why it is that many facts of which evidence is now abundant were unknown to Sir H. S. Maine, and how it is that the information available to that distinguished exponent of historical jurisprudence *seemed* to him so conclusive, and *was* really so imperfect, and in some respects misleading.[1] And when this has been explained, it will be proper to indicate the nature of the later and improved evidence that has become

[1] Sir H. S. Maine several times speaks of the completeness with which the Indian village had been observed; and though he suggests the need of re-examining the evidence on some points ("V. C.," pp. 12, 13), he betrays no sense that the evidence itself (in general) was deficient, and that the area covered by it was but small compared to the extent of all India. "No Indian phenomenon," he says ("V. C.," p. 103), "has been more carefully examined, and by men more thoroughly in earnest, than the Village Community." But this "observation" was from the administrative revenue point of view, and was very little directed to the history or ethnography of the villages. To anyone who has compared the documents available before (or about) 1870 with the materials since made accessible, Sir H. Maine's remark will appear truly astonishing.

available. Next, after some preliminary explanations regarding the agricultural population of India, I shall endeavour to account for the two separate forms of village (and the several varieties of one of the forms), and to show how they really came into existence. And then it will be desirable shortly to criticise the hitherto accepted *theory*, showing how it fails to satisfy the conditions in the case of either kind of village. Finally, I shall add a few general remarks on the subject of village ownership, and note some considerations suggested by the economic aspects of village life.

II

EXPLANATION OF TERMS

THERE are certain terms which must be made use of in this discussion, of which I had better at once interpolate an explanation; and this of itself will, perhaps, not be quite devoid of interest to anyone who cares to know about Indian economic conditions generally. One of them, the term *Village*, we have already more than once employed; and in speaking of village institutions it is hardly possible to avoid allusion to *tribes* or *clans* and their customs, for into such groups the Indian people once always were—and still are, in many cases—divided. Then, too, we shall often have occasion to allude to the *Revenue Settlement* and the *Settlement Report*. These three subjects may be shortly explained, by way of introduction to what follows, and this plan will avoid subsequently interrupting the course of argument by explanations.

What is a Village?

(1) First as to a *village*; the term does not refer merely to a street or group of buildings—as in England

of to-day; it includes both the cluster of houses and the surrounding lands cultivated. Such a group has always a local name and known limits. It is a fact that the level plains of India[1] were originally brought under cultivation *in groups* of holdings, each group ultimately, but not always at first, having defined boundaries, and covering from a few hundred to two or three thousand acres. It depends on the density of the agricultural population whether these groups are actually contiguous and cover the whole district like the squares of a chess-board, or whether they are more dispersed—stretches of barren waste, or jungle land dividing one from the other.

So much for the village *area*. But in all cases alike, the *body of persons* residing on, owning, or cultivating the land thus separately circumscribed, must necessarily tend to form, in some sense, a "community" more or less self-contained. In the first place the inhabitants reside together, very often in one central group of houses or cottages, built on an elevation at some convenient point within the village area.[2] Such a village dwelling-site is often surrounded

[1] There are certain places not only in the hill districts but also in the plains, where (from physical and climatic causes chiefly) village groups are not found. See "Ind. Vill. Comm.," p. 57 ff.

[2] In some cases the tendency, especially of later times, is for several small hamlets to be formed, or for small groups of farms to be scattered about. It will be understood that my description is very general, and that the form of building, of mud, brick, bamboo, thatch, tiles, etc., etc., varies extremely. I have

by mud walls, having gateways which lead into narrow and tortuous lanes. Outside is an open space, on which all the village cattle assemble in the evening, and where the village weavers stretch the webs for the cloth they are going to weave for local use. There is often a common "tank," or a pond, or a public well, for the general use; also the village temple, shrine, or mosque, as the case may be. Usually there is a small grove, or at least a spreading tree with a raised platform round it, which forms the common meeting place. Beside the dwellings of the principal landholders are also the cottages of dependents and subordinate tenants, as well as of the farm labourers, village servants, and artificers.[1]

The term "village servants" needs a word of elucidation. Every village is obliged to provide for itself the means of supplying the simple wants of life. The people could not go to a perhaps far

collected a number of notices of the subject in my "Ind. Vill. Comm.," pp. 67 ff.

[1] In South India, owing to caste arrangements, the village menials of low caste (or no caste at all) are kept together, just outside the villagers' dwellings. This fact has been noticed by Maine ("V. C.," p. 127)—one of the few places in which he mentions the villages of the south. But it is not, as he says, a matter of "certain villages," it is the universal feature in the Madras districts. It should be remembered, moreover, that the low caste menials, etc., of a northern village are not a bit more *part* of the "village community" than these southern out-castes; the "community" really consists of the "colonists and invaders" —the landowners of the village. This subject will be mentioned further in the sequel.

distant town to buy shoes or find a carpenter ; and hence they attract to themselves, and provide for, a little group (varying in different parts) of resident artificers and servants—a potter, a blacksmith, a cobbler, carpenter, washerman, sweeper, cattle-keeper, men to keep watch and ward, a barber to shave them (who also practises a rude kind of surgery and carries messages connected with betrothals), and so on. These servants live permanently in the village, and become hereditary ; they are not paid by the job[1] but work for every village resident for a fixed annual (or harvest) allowance of grain, cash, and perquisites. In some parts they have small holdings of rent-free land, which (like the duty itself) are hereditary.[2] So are the *village officers*, of whom I must next speak.

Provision has to be made for managing village affairs and local governance. And here it is that one of the fixed marks of distinction between two great classes of village, which will henceforth need to be distinguished, comes into view. In one class an important hereditary Headman (called *pâtêl* and by

[1] The persons requiring work done supply their own materials, or else pay for them ; there may be special customs in this respect.

[2] The institution of hereditary land attached to village service is chiefly observed (where it has survived at all) in that class of village which is prevalent in the Dakhan and the south of India. The remark ("V.C.," p. 126) that this form of payment is most common in the (joint) villages of the north (there referred to) is certainly not correct.

other names)[1] is an essential part of the constitution. He occupies a central building (in some places called the *garhi*, *i.e.*, fort); he has privileges of dignity and precedence on ceremonial occasions, and frequently a valuable holding of land (*watan*) which is his in virtue of hereditary office.[2] Such an officer is often assisted by executive deputies. In former days, the villages relied greatly on the protection given by this official: his moral influence, and even his material power (for he often had a considerable following), helped to keep oppression at bay. Certain it is that some vestige of old clannish loyalty[3] must

[1] It is stated in some books that the *pâtêl*, or headman, was first appointed by the ruler of the state. It is quite possible that in more recent times of Mughal and Mahrâtha domination, the governor may have assumed to make and unmake such appointments, for his own purposes; but that does not alter the fact that the headman is really an integral part of the village constitution; he was, in fact, the leader, the head of the eldest or chief family of the original settlers. It was the accountant, not the headman, whose office was added on by the state—to look after the revenue.

[2] See my "Ind. Vill. Com.," pp. 14, 15. Such holdings are now only locally intact; but the institution itself can be very widely traced. As a privileged holding it was naturally one very likely to become surcharged, and lost, in days of harsh revenue administration, and disregard of rights. Sir H. Maine ("V. C.," p. 123) speaks of the villages under headmen as cases that "frequently occur." This is hardly an adequate expression of the fact that this form is one that *uniformly prevails* over provinces aggregating more than half a million square miles in extent.

[3] I shall explain further on what is meant by these references to "tribe" or "clan."

be invoked to explain the attachment of the people to the old *pâtêlgî* family. If a ruler wished to restore cultivation in an abandoned village, he would hardly succeed without taking pains to trace out a genuine representative of the old *pâtêl's* family to head the returning party. If another headman had to be appointed, it was always understood that he would vacate the post directly a real descendant made his appearance.

But in another form of village, where the land-owning body is composed of a dominant class, holding the whole jointly or in shares, no such headman is found.[1] Village affairs are, or formerly were, controlled by a council of elders or heads of the co-sharing householders—all being equal in rank—not official chiefs.[2] The co-sharing families are in

[1] For official purposes connected with the Revenue, Police, etc., a headman (or one for each section of village) has been appointed, and the office has been allowed to become partly elective. This *lambar dâr* (as his half-English designation of "number-holder" indicates) is no part of the original constitution, but merely the agent or representative of the village in its dealings with the district authorities.

[2] Sir H. S. Maine has implied rather than stated that the council is the *original* universal form, and that where the headman is found it is a later change; see, for example, "V. C.," p. 123 and p. 154 (where he uses the phrase, "Even where the government *has passed* to one hereditary officer," etc.) There is no warrant for such a suggestion. If anything, it is the reverse; a village with a headman may become dominated by a joint-body, and the headman may disappear, or at least his distinctive position and authority may. Where the headman is found (all over peninsular India) he certainly has not super-

fact too jealous of their equal position to allow any one man to take the lead as the *pâtêl* of a Central Indian or Dakhan village did. But in both forms of village an "accountant and registrar" (*patwâri, kulkarni*, or *karnam*, etc., in the south) early became a necessity; because very probably hardly any other person could write or cast accounts. Such an official has, in the north, only a limited claim that his son should succeed him; and he may now (in some places) be transferred from one charge to another like an ordinary public officer.[1] But in the south the *karnam* is always hereditary, and is (or ought to be) reckoned as strictly belonging to his own village. There are also rural police or guardians

seded any other authority. It will be understood that the council or committee spoken of is the standing body—much more in evidence formerly than it is now—which manages the common affairs. A *panchâyat* or committee of elders for settling disputes is assembled in every form and condition of village, whether in the north or south, and quite independently of what the village constitution is. It was, and still is, to some extent, the universal Indian mode of settling caste, social and land cases, and especially boundary disputes. But the body (consisting only of members of the proprietary families) which once governed the joint-village is a standing committee for reference in all affairs of common interest. It is not a mere occasional assembly of elders, called together when there is a dispute, but the continuing and ordinary governing body as opposed to a single "headman," or the oligarchy of a few chiefs and officers.

[1] As a matter of fact, in the N.W.P. and Panjâb, in modern times, the *patwâri*, besides being trained and taught to survey, is in charge not of a single village, but of a "circle," which may include two or three villages.

of the village and its lands and boundaries, sometimes "trackers" to follow stolen cattle, and messengers who act under orders of the headman or other governing authority, as the case may be.[1]

I have hitherto only incidentally said anything about the nature of the connection which the *personnel* of the "village"—at least, the cultivating or landowning class—has with the soil. To do that more expressly, I again am obliged to distinguish between the two classes of village already intimated. Before I do so, let me emphasise the fact that *every* village (whatever its difference as regards the interest in the soil) is a more or less isolated group with its own officers, menials, etc., so that there must arise certain common interests; and the group is sure to develop a certain sense of solidarity, quite apart from any question of communal or collective ownership. The grouping of holdings in a more or less compact village form was a necessity of (permanent) agricultural establishment, under the early conditions of Indian life, both physical and social. Their comparative isolation resulted from similar causes. Where the population is sparse, it may be that the residents of a village rarely leave its neighbourhood; their own "community" is almost the only society known to them; the world beyond is strange. Often the land-

[1] For details as to village servants, and a certain classification of them according to rank, see "Ind. Vill. Comm.," pp. 17, 18.

owning class of one village is (at the present day) of a different tribe or caste to that of the next; and there may be no friendly feeling, if not a positive feud, between them. Everything tended to make each village self-contained, and to originate institutions that kept its caste, or family, or tribal connection (where such already existed) in remembrance. So far, and so far only, is there any unity of type which extends to all provinces alike.

But to return to the rights in the soil. Here we have two conditions marking two distinct classes or kinds of village. In one—which also is distinguished by the hereditary headman—there is no ownership of the whole village by a single proprietor, nor joint-ownership of it by a body of co-sharers, but the whole area is divided into a number of separate and independent holdings. Each separate holding may now have several sharers in it, because the families have long become "Hindus," and follow the joint-family custom; but the holdings themselves are separate and always were so, as far as any evidence goes. Indeed, by comparison with certain ancient but still surviving local customs, we are able (at least with probability) to account for this form of village, on its own basis of separately allotted holdings, as perhaps the earliest *organised* (though not the earliest *rudimentary*) form of permanent agricultural village in India.

In the other class of village we find the whole area

claimed (in shares) by a dominant class, who, in some cases, cultivate their own holdings (*e.g.*, the Jat villages of the Panjâb), but frequently have a body of tenants under them. Such tenants may be either the remnants and representatives of an original cultivating body dominated (under a variety of circumstances) by the present co-sharers, or may be dependents and settlers located by them. This class of village exhibits several varieties; and the principle of sharing is different in each variety.

Most commonly the proprietors hold their shares of the cultivated land separately; either a partition has taken place, or else the village may be in such a form that the shares or lots were always separate, and were so arranged from the first foundation. In the latter case, "the co-proprietorship" refers to the village site, or to any waste area which is still joint property. Indeed, in many cases the "joint ownership" chiefly survives in the joint responsibility for the revenue, which the whole body accepts, and in some other customs maintaining union. But in one class of these villages it may be that the entire area is held undivided. More commonly the cultivated land is divided, and the waste left in common. Where the village is still held undivided, it may be not only formally unpartitioned, but actually managed as a joint estate. These cases, however, are exceptional. The causes of such a state of things will be noticed hereafter, and I shall also explain in due course the different basis on which the shares of the members of the co-proprietary "brotherhood" are arranged in the different varieties of joint village. But I may take this opportunity of remarking that a not inconsiderable number of villages have become included in the class of joint or co-shared villages purely by reason of the application to them of the N.W. Provinces Revenue system (and its official forms and records).

One other point requires mention—regarding the waste land or grazing and woodland attached to (or adjacent to) a village. In villages in which there is no co-sharing body, the landholder's right is to his occupied holding only; there is no area of waste (for grazing or for future division and cultivation) made over as the joint property of the landholders. When an area of grazing land is available in the vicinity, the settlement officer will mark it off for the *use* of the villagers, but (like other unoccupied land) it remains the property of the State; and where part of such land is also available gradually to be brought under the plough, any resident in the village can apply to the local officer for a plot or "number," and get it on terms of engaging to pay the revenue assessed thereon. When we come (in the sequel) to inquire into the origin of this form of village, we shall consider the question whether, at an earlier time, a definite area of adjacent waste was ever considered to *belong* to the group which constituted the village.

But in the second great class of villages, the body, family, or group constituting the "community" of proprietors has always been acknowledged to have a uniform right over the *whole area* included in the village, whether cultivated or not. If the "waste" is permanently left as grazing ground, the joint right to it as such is undoubted; if it is such as will eventually be partitioned and brought under the plough, the owners of the village will usually share it in the same proportion, and on the same rule of sharing as applies to the cultivated area. In a joint village, in fact, the revenue survey always includes an area of waste (where there is any available) as part of the property of the joint body, and it is theirs to do what they like with; they may retain it as grazing ground, or divide it, clear the wood, and bring it under cultivation as they think fit.

In order briefly to distinguish the class of village in which there is no joint ownership from that in which there is something of the kind, I must use the rather uncouth terms SEVERALTY village[1] and

[1] In my "Ind. Vill. Comm." I called it "*raiyatwâri*" village, that being the official term for the separate tenure. Here I want to avoid the use of technical terms as far as possible. I take the opportunity of noting that when a *vernacular* name is added in brackets, it is either because it will be useful to readers familiar with India or because the word itself (*e.g.*, *pâtêl*, *patwâri*, etc.) occurs in English books.

JOINT village. I should like to call the latter "manorial villages"—the village become subject to some kind of "overlordship,"[1] as it so often is; but the term would only accurately fit one class of cases, and, moreover, would sound too strange, at any rate in the present stage of the discussion.

It may be convenient to summarise the *salient features* of difference between the two kinds of village in a short table:—

I. SEVERALTY (or *Raiyatwâri*) VILLAGE	II. JOINT VILLAGE
1. Influential headman (often still possessing certain privileges) is part of the natural constitution.	1. No headman originally, but a *panchâyat.* In modern times an official headman, appointed to represent the community.
2. Holdings entirely separate, and not shares of a unit estate.	2. The holdings (sometimes joint) are shares of a unit estate.
3. No joint liability for revenue: each holding separately assessed on its merits.	3. Liability (joint and several) always, for the revenue assessed in a lump sum.
4. No jointly owned area of waste or "common" land belongs to the village, or is available for partition.	4. The village site, and usually an area of waste, owned in common, and is available for partition.

The severalty village, with its hereditary headman, is the prevalent form over the whole of Bengal (ex-

[1] By "overlordship" (here and elsewhere) I do not mean a defined political or "feudal" superiority; I use the word solely as a conveniently wide term for any kind of virtual superiority by which one man (or one class) is able to exact submission, or to take rent, from another.

cluding Bihâr), over Central India, and the West and South;[1] while there is reason to believe it was once prevalent in such parts of Northern India as were earliest cultivated, until the conquering tribes and landlord families changed the constitution, and the joint form grew up. However that may be, it is a plain matter of fact that the joint village is confined, *i.e.*, as the prevalent type, to the north of India—from the Indus as far east as Bihâr, though it is (or was once) found locally, and under special circumstances, elsewhere. In this preliminary account of what is meant by "village," and dealing only with matters of fact and observation, I will not include anything as to the causes of the difference between the tenure of Northern India and that of the peninsula.

[1] As I noted that the severalty village is prevalent over an area of more than half a million square miles, I may add here that the "joint" form is characteristic in about 200,000 square miles. It is worth while adding that all over the country of the severalty villages there are a variety of local indigenous names for the headman (*mundâ*, *mandal*, *pâtêl*, *gauda*, *reddî*, etc.). Throughout the N.W. Provinces, Panjâb, etc., on the contrary, where the joint form (without a headman) has long prevailed, the local dialects have no current word for "headman," the only term in use being either an Arabic word introduced by the Mughal Revenue Administration or the half-English word "*lambar-dâr*" (= "holder of a number") belonging to the British system.

Tribes and Clans in India

(2) There is one other matter connected with Indian villages, and the Indian population generally, which gives rise sometimes to no little misapprehension. In Europe, at the present day, we live out of all contact with "tribes" or "clans"; we know of them only in history, or in distant countries, and they have become the subject of theories as to their origin and principle of association; and so we regard the mention of them with some suspicion.[1] But in Upper India (especially) we live every day in close proximity with people actually forming "tribes" or "clans," which are either small and independent groups or (frequently) sections of a larger "tribe." And even where the whole social constitution on tribal lines is not kept up, still we feel sure the people must have formed tribes and clans at no very remote period, for they still use a common designation, and record themselves at a census, or other occasion, as of such-and-such a "tribe," although they may have forgotten much of the customary life which would have made the "tribe" a reality. But whether in

[1] For example, use is made of the term "tribe," although the original may be only such a word as *populus*. There is no such mistake in India; there are distinct words for the tribe, the clan (or other subdivision), and the family. In the north the common term for a whole tribe is *qaum* (borrowed from the Arabic), while a division or clan is *gôt*; and there are other terms (given in "Ind. Vill. Comm.," p. 194).

perfection or decay, the tribe or clan is quite a real thing in India; in some parts more so than others. We have also "codes" of custom, of which a notable feature is that they apply to *tribes*, not to *places*, and are often different in detail.

In modern life we soon forget any family connection beyond one or two generations. A "family" we recognise as consisting of the head of the household and his children, and possibly grandchildren; perhaps (collaterally) a certain number of brother's or sister's children, and even second cousins, are pretty closely connected. But in those parts of India in which there are recognised "clans," and especially where the clan is known to be a section of a larger "tribe," we find that the people invariably recognise consanguinity, and even though in some cases this may be partly fictitious, *i.e.*, various elements have been associated only, still the people believe in their descent from a common ancestor. In other words, the feeling of kindred is diffused over a much wider circle than the unit "family."

It is evident, from a variety of literary and traditional evidence, that the early Aryan and other races invading India formed "tribes" with a certain organisation; and we infer also from the existing forms of village and land customs and from the names used, and traditions preserved, that such (later) races as the Jats, Râjputs, and Gujars, were also settled under the rules of tribal life, some of which they still observe. And lastly to those "tribes" of which we have the evidence before our eyes, we find two conditions which are established. (1) We find a single group—possessing lands in one place or in more than one—but not known to be a subdivision of any larger body. (2) We find a whole tribe, with its major and minor, and ultimate, subdivisions all complete.

In the first case, the existing group remembers only its descent from some one ancestor, and is not numerous enough to be called a "tribe." In all probability one man (or two or three brothers) obtained a settlement in some region that was vacant, and the families multiplied into a "clan," keeping up the memory of their common descent and acknowledging a certain solidarity. Among the Râjputs or other tribes which had adopted a monarchical constitution, it is common to find that the ancestor became the *Râjâ* and that the heads of the branch families held subordinate (territorial) titles (as *Râwal*, *Thâkur*, etc.), and there was a regularly understood method of territorial rule in the Râjâ's central dominion and those of the other chiefs lying round. The subjects of each were bound to allegiance to the chief, and the chief to the Râjâ. On sending round the message for assembly (*gohar*) every member of the clan able to bear arms would at once join the chief's standard.

On the north-western frontier of the Panjâb we can observe not only "clans" like those of the Râjputs or Jats, but a wider organisation. We find a whole tribe, and its "clans" which are the larger sections; and there are again smaller sections. Here the constitution is not monarchical—the chiefs are not princes or Râjâs. We observe this organisation both with reference to the *land* occupied, and also to the grouping of the *people* who have settled on the land and divided it among themselves. It is not always certain that such bodies are descended from one ancestor; but it is traditionally asserted and believed, and often the genealogical tree is preserved. It is indeed often the case that other tribes have been taken into association (*hamsâya*) as protected; and lands have been given them by the principal tribe; but they are not regarded as amalgamated, nor is the separate descent forgotten. Among the north-western frontier tribes, I may refer to one instance in the Yusafzai country, where there is the domain (*ilâqa*) of a single tribe; every member of it knows that he is descended from one ancestor, who, if he were alive, would be the revered patriarch of their whole body. Beyond that, and the fact that their land is all in one great territory, the *tribe* happens to be not so marked as the several primary divisions or *clans*. Of these there are three; and their territory is in three great contiguous blocks. Each such territory is made into large secondary sections called *tappa*. (The first contains two, the second two, and the third five.) Ordinarily these *tappa* territories correspond to a group of descendants whose designation ends with the syllable-*zai* (which in the local language [Pashtu] means "son of"). The *tappa* is finally divided into a number of "companies" (or *Khel*). The *Khel* is a group usually much larger than a "village."[1] In the course of time what with the convenience of the administration requiring it, and the growth of separate hamlets with their cultivation lying adjacent, "villages" are gradually formed, and separately demarcated.

On the other hand it may sometimes happen, though the appearance of a clan is less perfect, that we find a large extent of country containing several hundred square miles, now divided up into "village" groups, all composed of landowners whose families have a common designation and are reputed descendants of one ancestor; or of two or three families, not more.[2] In such cases it is often difficult to say whether the existing group originally came (in smaller number, but still as a group) and divided the land according to their requirements at the time, or whether two or three adventurers formed little settlements in the abundant waste, and in the course of a couple of centuries or more, multiplied into the existing large group.

As regards the *personal* connection, in a tribe or clan, it is kept up and acknowledged far beyond the

[1] There is an account of this very perfect example of clan territories, and a diagram which makes the arrangement visible at one glance, in "Ind. Vill. Comm.," pp. 247-9.

[2] For example see the same work, p. 271.

limits within which we are accustomed ourselves to remember it. It takes effect in rules of marriage, by which a man or a woman of one group cannot marry one of the same group, but must go to another. It also produces a willingness of the whole body to act, for defence or offence, in unison, and for convenient groups to undertake a joint-responsibility (for example) for a total sum of land tax on the entire area, so as to preserve the villages from an inquisition by a tax gatherer. It produces a willing obedience to the "custom" of the tribe regarding adoption, the non-alienation of land and other matters. Lastly, it produces a strong sense that every member of the "clan" (or whatever group circumstances have kept together) has his right to share in the land acquired by the adventure and settlement—perhaps by the conquest of the whole body. And if the tribal system is fully maintained, it is a feature that as the clan expands, the heads of the eldest branches or principal families, and (in turn) the heads of subordinate families, should be known by their appropriate titles, as chiefs of the clan, of the sub-clan, of the still smaller section, and so forth.[1] The authority of these *chiefs* may be greater or less, and may extend to certain concerns of life only; but where it survives there is a very distinct sentiment of loyalty, and

[1] Usually the chief is the eldest (competent) member of the eldest branch; but the chiefship may be transferred to some other member for any special reason.

obedience is unquestioned. When, therefore, it is mentioned (for example) that in the "severalty" village of the Dakhan, the loyalty with which the headman's family is still regarded is a relic of the clan spirit, I mean nothing more than that originally the village was formed by a small section of a then existing organised clan, that the "village head" was the hereditary leader of that particular section; that he was loyally obeyed owing to that spirit of allegiance which is well known to everyone who (for instance) has read about the Highland clans of Scotland.

It is possible (in itself) that a "clan," etc., may be constituted on a *matriarchal* basis or a *patriarchal*. It may be that all descendants of a common mother form the essential group; but all the more advanced tribes that we know of in India in connection with organised village settlements (and often under monarchical rule)—such as the later Dravidian people of the centre and south, or the Jats, Râjputs, and frontier tribes in the north—are all clearly patriarchal: descent, chiefship, and inheritance all go with the fathers of the expanding family. Some further remarks on this subject will be made hereafter.

There is therefore no hidden assumption or doubtful theory involved in our allusion to the "tribe" or "clan" with reference to Indian peasant landholding; it means nothing more than we know, or at least have the strongest reason to infer, from all the facts of the case.

I will repeat that the degree of preservation in which "clans," or aggregates of clans forming tribes, exist is various; and in parts of India such an organisation has been quite forgotten; perhaps what was once the name of a *tribe* has now become a *caste* name. But the existence of such tribal organisation has had a great deal to do both with village formation and with the constitution of the Hindu state.

I have indicated the fact (and without entering into details) that some tribes developed a system of King or Râjâ and subordinate chiefs in a sort of "feudal" service, out of the patriarch of the tribe and the chiefs of its sections. This often happened with the Râjputs; but some Râjputs (like the Bisên Clan of Oudh) did not adopt the system. In fact, whatever may be the reason, some Indian clans or tribes acknowledged the King and "barons" (who were the chiefs of elder and younger branches of the stock), others did not.

It will more conveniently appear at a later stage how tribal life and the allotment of lands to the members has produced certain forms of village community.

The Land-Revenue Settlement

We have mentioned incidentally the assessment of the amount of land-revenue which is payable to the State by these villages. That assessment is (in modern times) imposed by means of an operation called a "Land-Revenue Settlement." What has such a Settlement to do with the constitution and form of villages, and what is the "Settlement Report"?

It is probably known to most readers that in India the State has, from very ancient times, relied for its chief source of revenue on the right or claim to receive a portion of the produce of all cultivated land. At first this share was levied (and still is so in some of the remoter native states) *in kind;* but in all the greater provinces, it had, for many generations before British rule, frequently been converted into a cash assessment calculated at a certain rate per "plough" (*i.e.*, the area worked by one plough), or per local standard measure (*bîghâ*, etc.) according to value and advantage of the different kinds of soil. In some cases it was very oppressively levied, and swallowed up nearly the whole "rent" or profits of the holding, so that land-holding was an employment which was often a burden, and left the holder no more than a bare living. Under British rule, it early became a principal object to assess this demand equally, and at such moderate rates as would leave a substantial profit or surplus; at the same time determining who were the persons to be responsible for payment and entitled to take, or at least to participate in, the profits of the holding. The classification and valuation of land for the purposes of assessment, as well as the inquiry into rights, which are the chief objects of a Revenue Settlement or Survey Settlement, have always been duties requiring skill and experience, and have always been entrusted to a class of selected officers known as "Settlement officers." Their work in the field began with a detailed survey and a record, village by village, of every field and holding. Such a survey was not only necessary for valuation purposes, but equally so for making a record of rights and interests of all kinds in the soil.[1] Each provincial system varies in detail, inasmuch as the mode of assessment and the fixing of the revenue demand, whether on a whole estate on a whole village, or on an individual field, is different. And the system is adapted in each province to suit the prevalent land tenure. It follows that, directly or indirectly, the survey and the inquiry tend to make known the whole features of village constitution and history, especially if the officer in charge interests himself in the subject. I will only remark here that the variation between the *joint-village*, as I have described it in the northern provinces, and the *severalty* (or

[1] The Bombay and Madras systems do not *profess* to inquire into rights; but under the *raiyatwâri* tenure, there prevalent, the record of every holding and part holding of the *ryot* and his relatives forms as good a record of right and title as could be desired. There was also one Settlement made (1789-93) in Bengal in which there was no survey; but that was under peculiar circumstances; and the plan of dispensing with a survey was never adopted elsewhere as a general system.

raiyatwâri) in others, has been the cause of the difference between two prominent forms of Revenue Administration.

When the whole process of a "Settlement" is over, and the term[1] for which the assessment is to hold good (without increase) is fixed, the officer in charge draws up (in English) a report on his proceedings. Speaking now of the "reports" of the N.W. Provinces and some of the adjoining (and then included) south-eastern districts of the Panjâb, it may be explained that at the *first* settlements, time pressed, administration was less elaborate, and it was of more importance to give only the salient features of the actual revenue arrangements made. But when, in these provinces, the first—rather tentative—settlements expired and a new series of district settlements began, the second (in some cases later than the second) series of reports (dated after 1870) were much fuller and more complete. Nor will any future revision of the assessment require the repetition of such detailed survey and other information. The past history of the district is given; its climate, soil, local features, and even its antiquities are described; the origin, history, and customs of the principal castes and tribes are recorded; and (what more especially concerns us) the details of village

[1] Usually for thirty years; but the Government settles that on a variety of considerations; no term is fixed by law.

history and the peculiarities of tenure-customs, and the nature and growth of the village proprietary bodies—when and how they were established—are examined in detail. All these matters have an obvious if more or less direct bearing on the condition of the people, on the question of their rights and interests, and on the proper classification and assessment of their holdings. Hence the "Settlement Reports," when they belong to the later period of complete record are, though of course in varying degrees of excellence, veritable mines of information.

III

THE EVIDENCE REGARDING VILLAGES BEFORE AND AFTER 1870

NOW let us briefly glance at the evidence which was available before 1870 regarding village institutions; why it gave so much prominence to the idea of "common holding," and why it was calculated to suggest that uniformity existed (far more than it really exists) throughout India.[1]

Sir H. S. Maine came to India at the end of 1862, as member of the Viceregal Council in charge of the Legislative Department; he remained till the end of 1869. His high duties confined his residence chiefly to Calcutta (in Bengal), which is the winter-capital of the Government of India, and to Simla in the Panjâb Hills. On the way between one and the

[1] In speaking of the defective evidence and of the great improvement that has since taken place, I should like to call to mind how much we owe to Sir H. S. Maine for the example of his aim and method, and for the stimulus that his works gave to inquiries which resulted in the later reports and monographs. It is only fair to remember that it is to this pioneer work that we are largely indebted for the superior character and fulness of the later records.

C

other lies Allâhâbâd, the capital of the North-Western Provinces. Now in Bengal the village system—whatever its original form—had become almost completely overborne by the growth of the great middlemen or "Zamîndârs," whom Lord Cornwallis had acknowledged as the "actual proprietors" of estates. At any rate, Bengal did not afford many opportunities for gathering information regarding village institutions. But in the North-West Provinces, Oudh, and the Panjâb, the village system was not only flourishing as, in fact, the prevailing tenure feature of the country, but the villages were held by co-sharing bodies, sometimes of one family, and often of the same tribe or clan; they were of that type which has already been indicated in general terms as the "joint village." Sir H. S. Maine's attention was necessarily, almost exclusively, directed to this region. It was to it that a great part of the more specific evidence at his disposal related; and it happened, during his years of office, that special questions regarding the law of tenants and subordinate landholders in these parts of India were awaiting treatment by the Legislature. And when I say that a great deal of the evidence available before 1870 directly related to the Northern Provinces, it should be added that the more famous official minutes and published accounts of "the village," though couched in general terms, and without indicating any particular locality, were chiefly based on the same northern form of village. Indeed, before 1870 but little specific information regarding India south of the Narbada was available. The Revenue Settlement surveys of the Dakhan or Bombay Presidency[1] were still in progress, and very little was known, outside the Presidency, about the matter. There is indeed an excellent sketch of the Dakhan village, in Elphinstone's History, which Sir H. S. Maine must have read; but it is unfortunately mixed up with some details about the other forms of village, and altogether is not such as to induce a reader already disposed to believe in a unity of type, to discover the real difference. Indeed it is a common fault in Indian books which give an account of "the village," that they take various particulars from different places and combine them all in one general picture. Of the "Central Provinces" some of the (then recent) Settlement Reports must have been available; but a large part of the country was settled on a very artificial principle, and the documentary evidence turned chiefly on questions connected with that, so that the real form and history of the local village hardly received any notice. Of Madras—the great Southern province, where the population is of non-Aryan origin, and where the original customs are different from those of the north—hardly anything was on record, or at least known to residents in

[1] In Bombay there was a long period of tentative revenue administration, and a complete system of survey-settlement was only brought into practice from about 1847.

Upper India.[1] The evidence available to Sir H. Maine really applied to Hindustân or Upper India, and even then it did not, I think, give him more than a very limited idea of the Panjâb villages.[2] The connection of the village and the tribe, so prominently illustrated in that province, never seems to have come to his notice.

The evidence, in short, consisted of (1) the Settlement Reports of the N.W. Provinces, and, perhaps, the Panjâb; and (2) of official minutes and orders, among

[1] Once Sir H. Maine refers ("E. H. I.," p. 71) to a volume entitled "Mirâsi Papers," which relates to Madras; but the question there treated is of a special kind, and would not enlighten anyone about Madras villages in general.

[2] I could easily show from Sir H. S. Maine's works that he had not been informed about the tribal villages in the Panjâb frontier districts, or the features of the Jat villages in the plains. One passage ("E. H. I.," p. 83) shows clearly that the village area known to the author was the comparatively densely populated region of the N.W. Provinces and Oudh; for in remarking on an interesting phenomenon of village growth, namely, the expansion of a single village into a number, by throwing off small derivative groups who form hamlets in the adjacent waste, in time producing a whole circle of villages, he says that this is *not* exhibited by "the Indian communities placed in a region of which the population has been from time immemorial far denser," etc. Had the author been acquainted with the central and S.E. Panjâb—not to mention other places—he could not have penned such a remark, for the population is not at all dense, and the multiplication of villages in this very way is quite a characteristic feature, and, indeed, is one of the most important causes of what are, or appear to be, clan-settlements or groups of villages all of one descent.

which I may mention Thomason's celebrated "Directions to Settlement Officers." [1]

It is not necessary to speak at any length of these documents, familiar to Indian readers, but strange to any others. It is only necessary to point out their insufficiency, and to note that they had a special character which would foster the idea that "common ownership" was a characteristic of villages in general. As regards (1) the Settlement Reports mentioned, they are only those of the first (or at all events earlier) Settlements in the N.W. Provinces. Having recently looked over some of them, I was almost surprised to see how imperfect they are—imperfect, that is, for the purpose of enlightenment about the true history of the villages. They take for granted the rough and highly unsatisfactory official classification of villages which the "Circular Orders" of the Revenue authorities had adopted—and to do them justice, had adopted merely for official purposes, as briefly embodying the distinctions that were useful from an administrative point of view. They are

[1] The author also speaks of verbal information; this, of course, cannot be criticised except to the extent of saying that it was not likely to be much in advance of the standard of published information available at the time.

I have not included any mention of books like Tod's "Rajasthan," or the writings of Colonel Wilks, Sir J. Malcolm, Grant-Duff, or Dr. Buchanan. No use seems to have been made of these works. And, indeed, though valuable materials for village history may here and there be found in them, it is not always apparent, and has to be disinterred from other subject-matter.

more concerned with describing the practical financial features of the assessments than with giving any kind of detailed information as to village custom. As to published Reports of the Panjâb districts, I can find no indication of Sir H. Maine's having made use of the more valuable of the first series, such as those on the Jihlam, Multân, or Gujrât districts.

As to (2) the official minutes, some of these (*e.g.* Sir C. Metcalfe's)[1] are picturesque rather than definitely instructive; others are conceived in general terms, and do not refer to any local details. It must be borne in mind that none of them were written for any purpose other than that of recommending certain practical measures; that they relate only to such localities as the authors were familiar with. They were not intended to be generally or universally applied. Moreover, many great names in India, like those of LAWRENCE, THOMASON, or MUNRO,[2] justly carry weight as regards their opinions; but it does not follow that those eminent administrators

[1] This well-known minute is given at p. 68 of the sixth edition of Elphinstone's "History of India."

[2] Sir John (afterwards Lord) Lawrence had been Collector of Delhi in the forties, and had done some Settlement work there, and was afterwards Chief Commissioner of the Panjâb, and ultimately Governor-General of India. Mr. Jas. Thomason was the founder of the improved Revenue Administration of the N.W. Provinces (1830-42), and afterwards was Lieutenant-Governor (1843). Sir T. Munro was the great advocate of the Madras Revenue System, and was made Governor of the Province (1820)

had either the time or the inclination to acquire or perfect the sort of information about village history, the origin of customs, and the course of clan movements, which is what is wanted for the special purpose of economic and historic inquiry. Hence their minutes must not be taken for more than their actual scope warrants. I can hardly, perhaps, include the late Sir G. Campbell's clever essay called "The Tenure of Land in India" (in the "Cobden Club Papers") as an official document, but it is alluded to by Sir H. S. Maine,[1] who recognises that it does not profess to give any detailed information. Indeed, village institutions are only very lightly and discursively touched on. The object is rather to describe the land-revenue management in general, than to explain the facts about the villages. The same may be said for the "Directions," which, invaluable as they were as the first systematic guide to revenue practice that had appeared, contain only a few brief (and very obscure) paragraphs explaining how the joint villages should be classified for purposes of record and revenue management.

But most of these sources of information had one feature which I must notice: they laid stress on one point—the "joint-ownership," or else on the sense of unity manifested by the villages, peculiarities which were specially important from an official point of view, as making it possible for them to be held

[1] "V. C.," p. 106.

jointly liable for one sum of revenue assessed on the whole village.[1] This recognition of the village as a sort of proprietary unit is the distinctive feature of the special N.W.P. Land-Revenue System. It will be remembered that when Bengal was permanently settled in 1793, the great desire of the Administration was to put an end to the theory that Government (or the State) was the sole and absolute owner of the land; and to find for each estate some private landlord, who would at once be liable for the revenue demand, and also assure the well-being of the cultivators on the estate. Now when the work of settling the revenue extended to what were then known as the "Ceded and Conquered districts" (the N.W. Provinces) in the beginning of the nineteenth century, there were (in most cases) no landlords suitable to be recognised, but there were the independent co-sharing village bodies. At first the idea was that some *one* proprietor or landlord must be recognised for each; and it took all the ability of Mr. Holt-Mackenzie (Secretary to the Revenue Commission) to convince the authorities that the whole village ought to be regarded as a "corporate" body or unit, which, being jointly responsible, could be treated with through a representative. The landlord principle was saved:

[1] This sum the co-proprietors distribute among themselves (so that the amount payable by each is known), according to the custom and constitution of the village. The process is known as the *bâchh*.

the joint body is the (ideal) landlord between the individual co-sharer and the State. Hence the joint constitution of these bodies is the theme of minutes and orders. An inquirer, pressed with such evidence, would easily conceive that "collective ownership" was *the* feature of villages, and that this must surely be the ancient common ownership that was believed to be universal. Add to this that in those days almost everyone believed that "Aryans" constituted the bulk of the population throughout India, so that what was true of one part would be true of another, and the idea of uniformity appears quite natural.

Since 1870 the new Settlement Reports gradually came in. We have them now for the whole of the Panjâb, North-West Provinces and Oudh, Âjmêr and the Central Provinces. We have excellent information on the tenures of Bengal, including the most interesting part of it—the "Chota Nagpore" districts. We have a series of valuable "District Manuals" for all the Madras districts; and in Bombay the published volumes of the *Gazetteer* enter fully into the tenures, and have, in fact, reproduced most of the material that is of importance in the local Settlement Reports and the special reports, such as those of Pottinger, Chaplin, Gooddine, Pedder, and others.[1]

[1] I have purposely said nothing about the great advance in ethnographical knowledge, and in the editing of coins and inscriptions which throw light on early history and the dynastic changes and tribal movements that India has witnessed.

IV

A GENERAL VIEW OF THE AGRICULTURAL RACES OF INDIA

BEFORE we can form an opinion about the history of Indian villages, and the value of theories propounded about them, it is desirable to glance generally at the agricultural population of India, as far as its origin is known or can be inferred with reasonable probability, from the literary, traditional, and linguistic evidence in our possession. Too much importance has probably been attributed to the Aryan immigration—in this sense at least, that it is, or used to be, regarded as furnishing the principal element in the entire population. But if one thing is more certain than another, it is that with the original "village" settlements of a large part of India, Aryans had nothing whatever to do.

The geographical features which are necessarily alluded to in speaking of the population and its movements are not difficult to keep in mind. The great Himalayan range (merging at the western end into the Hindu Kush mountains) forms a northern barrier; and the principal passes from Central Asia leading to India are in the north-west corner, beyond Peshâwar and Kâbul. Other passes into India cross the western frontier mountains (known as the Sulaimân) from Bilûchistân. Quite at the other end of Upper India, at the north-east, there is another route of access to races, who certainly found their way in that direction—races of a more Tibetan character. It is generally allowed that the ARYAN tribes came from the north-west passes; and by those on the west, in all probability, the TURANIAN (or Dravidian) races entered India. The TIBETO-BURMAN people of the outer Himalyan hills, and the ancient people called "KOLARIAN," both came from the north-east.

Let us note also, for convenience of reference, that India, as a whole, may be divided into two great portions—one called Hindustân, or "Upper" or "Northern" India, which (going from west to east), includes the Indus Valley, the Panjâb Plains, then the Ganges Valley (and Oudh), and then Bengal and Bihâr, and Assam beyond. This great expanse of plain country at the foot of the Himalaya is, roughly speaking, bounded on the south by a double range of hills of great breadth and intricacy, though of nothing like the height of the Himalaya. This group of hill ranges (of many local names) we generalise (for convenience) under the name of the "Vindhyan Hills." Through the middle of the ranges, and traversing a large part of the whole breadth of the continent from east to west, flows the great Narbada river in its broad and fertile valley. This "Vindhyan" and Narbada "line" separates completely (and did so in ancient times more effectually than at present), the people of the Dakhan, and Hyderabad, and the South, from any extensive immigration from "Upper" India. This great barrier, however, terminates before touching the west coast, and so leaves an open way for any tribes who came down the Indus Valley, to reach the Upper Dakhan or Bombay territory — Gujarât and the Mahrâtha country.

These features can easily be followed on a good general map, especially one of the mountain maps in the "Statistical Atlas of India," or in those attached to the periodical Parliamentary Blue-book on the "Moral and Material Progress of India." They had undoubtedly a great effect in directing and controlling the movements of the tribes who came to India in ancient times—the Aryan and Dravidian, and (so-called) Kolarian races; and also, later, Turanian races, and still later Indo-Scythian (Su or Abâr, the Yuechi or Kushân and Hûna) tribes,[1] who came in historic times, but at various dates, roughly speaking,

[1] Their history is well traced in the Archæol. Reports for North India, Vol. II., for instance, They gave rise (however indirectly and by mixture of race) to the local tribes in Upper India, known as Bâla, Ahîr, Ghakar, Jat (or Jât), Mer, and Gujar (Gurjar). Many of their leading families, too, became known as "Râjput."

between the sixth century B.C. and the sixth century A.D.

For a long time it was generally supposed that the ARYAN (Sanskrit speaking) people coming from the north-west through the passes just mentioned (much as Alexander the Great did several centuries later), settled in India; and that, in the course of their advance, they met with some insignificant black and snub-nosed "aboriginal" tribes, whom they defeated and drove out, either to a refuge in the outer Himalaya, or to the hills in the centre and upper South of India. From that time the Aryan (or at least a mixed Aryan) race formed the chief or predominating element in the population throughout India.

But such an idea can no longer be entertained. The literary allusions, traditions, and a number of ethnological and local circumstances, when better understood, compel us to the conclusion that the Aryans were a limited but very superior class: that they established themselves in "Hindustan" or Upper India, only locally extending beyond it on the west, and (after some time) on the eastern side also. Their establishment was, however, so important an event that we will return to trace its history a little more in detail presently.

Southern and Western India were peopled chiefly by TURANIAN or DRAVIDIAN tribes (the name is from *Dravira*, the Sanskrit form of the local name of South India).

Even the great Northern Indian plain was not occupied, or brought under cultivation for the first time, by the Aryans. There were besides the "barbarian" enemies mentioned in early literature[1] other (more advanced) tribes who most probably preceded the Aryans, and perhaps were nearly contemporaneous with them in the time of their settlement. These were also almost certainly of TURANIAN or DRAVIDIAN origin, the same as those of the west and south. Their language was different from that of the Aryans, and so remains all over the *south country* where its dialects (Tamil, Telugu, etc.) have only been moderately affected by the Sanskrit terms or grammatical forms afterwards introduced by the Brahmans. In *Northern India*, however, the Dravidian was gradually overborne—as a distinct element—by the Aryan and other later coming races (of whom we shall say a word presently). Such early Turanians as were in Upper India, therefore, became fused with these other races so that no trace of a separate language has survived. There are good reasons for believing that the earliest Turanian or Dravidian races originally came from the west frontier—perhaps by the Bolân and other western passes—while the Aryans came from the further north-west. One part (perhaps the chief bulk) of the Dravidian tribes then

[1] And who (considering the countries known to the writers of the Vedic hymns) must have been rude people in the north-western hills and the Northern Panjâb.

went down the Indus valley and across Gujarât to the west coast districts, and thence spread over the Dakhan and Madras. Perhaps some of them went by sea from the Indus mouth to the west coast. Whether the Dravidians who went into Upper India, and so became cut off from intercourse with those below the Vindhyan line of hills, came at the same time, only that they kept to Northern India and struck due east instead of going south, can only be a matter of speculation. But while the latter in time merged into the general Hindu population as above stated, the Southern Dravidians never were disturbed by any extensive immigration in after times, and so multiplied, and retained a distinctive character, though they accepted Hindu caste and religious teaching from Brahmans, who with their love of ascetic, hermit life, soon began to make their way south. Only the tribes in the west of India (upper part of Bombay) became much "Aryanised"; at least we conclude so, because the language of the west country was influenced by the speech of the Aryan tribes who penetrated by the Indus route; and the western languages (Marâthi and Gujarâti) became distinct both from those of the south and those of Upper India. But these early Dravidians of prehistoric times were not the only representatives of the stock in India. Besides the first races, who were serpent worshippers[1] (at least many tribes were), other races of the same

[1] Indicated by the names in literature—*Ahi*, *Nâga*, etc.

stock, but of other branches perhaps, continued to come to Upper, and even Eastern Central India (in later times); and showed themselves possessed of a strongly organised system of government, which has been likened to the "feudal" system of Europe.[1]

Besides the Dravidian races, another less numerous series, with a different language called (not very happily) KOLARIAN, had in very early times come to India, as I have said, from the north-eastern corner; and some who are called TIBETO-BURMAN—confined, however, to Assam and to the districts along the outer slopes of the Himalaya.

Naturally, there are a number of small local tribes, now in a very backward condition, who are generally spoken of as "aboriginal," and whose classification is uncertain. And the earlier Dravidians and Kolarians became mixed up together in some localities in a perplexing manner. The Dravidians, regarded as forming the general population of

[1] We know that there was an ancient serpent (and sun) worshipping race in Kashmir; that the people of Taxila, in Alexander's time, were snake worshippers, and certainly not Aryans. It is possible that the known invasions about the time of Darius Hystaspes (sixth century B.C.) brought new Turanian tribes to North India. A Turanian royal family appears about that time to have succeeded to the earlier Aryan dynasty of the Magadha kingdom (E. Bengal). From them are derived the Andhra, who at one time dominated the upper part of the peninsula, and also the Nâga or Snake Kings of Eastern Central India. These later invasions were of clans probably identical in race with the earliest Dravidians ("snakes" or *Ahi*) of epic times.

SOUTHERN INDIA, have been slowly changed in the course of ages by climate and locality, and by accepting caste and the Hindu religion and customs. So that we do not expect to find their village and other customs actually primitive, but only showing some marks of their origin. But there are places in Chota Nagpore, Orissa, and elsewhere, where some Dravidian tribes have retained their original customs. From these we can find out what was in all probability the earliest form of village. And we have traces both of an earlier village and of a later and much more organised form, which latter we naturally attribute to the latest rather than to the earliest Turanian immigrants.

It is only reasonable to believe that the Dravidians in NORTHERN INDIA had very much the same kind of villages. So that the ruling and superior Aryans when they came to Northern India found, at least in parts of the Panjâb and in the more fertile regions of the Ganges valley, cultivation already established. There is every reason to believe that even the earliest Dravidians were agriculturists by nature; and certainly the later, but still ancient, tribes knew how to form well ordered villages and to allot lands, and how to make forts and buildings and to prepare reservoirs or *tanks* for irrigation.[1]

[1] It is worth while noting that "tank" is not the English word, giving the idea of a great vessel of iron plates bolted together, but means a partly natural, partly artificial, reservoir,

Now let us very briefly notice what happened when the ARYANS began to spread over the plains of India, leaving behind them some of their families and allies in the north-west hills—*e.g.*, in Kashmir, and the country north of Peshâwar—only to mention fairly familiar names.

When the ARYAN tribes appeared in the plains of UPPER INDIA, the earliest Vedic hymns give us some idea of their movement. And later literature carries on, so to speak, the story of their establishment. One part of the tribes is represented as occupying the Indus valley. Another and larger part made its way across the Panjâb towards the south-east to the Jamna river and the Ganges plain; they extended thence eastward, coming at last as far as the mouths of the Hûghli river and to Assam. These indications are confirmed in various ways.[1] The two sections so separated had a different history and development. The former—largely composed of a tribe "Yâdava" (sons of Yadu) can be traced spreading southwards beyond the Indus valley (and adjacent parts of the West Panjâb) till they reached Gujarât (North Bombay) and the Mahrâtha country. The latter group—probably much the larger—dominated the whole of the Doâb and the Ganges plain; they were

and is derived from a native (Dravidian) word of something the same sound.

[1] For example by traditions, local remains, existence of linguistic traces, and a number of other coincident circumstances.

separated by the dry Panjâb plains from the Indus valley tribes (and from such as extended thence into the West Panjâb), and were cut off from peninsular India, to the south and west, by the ranges of the Vindhyan hill series and the Narbada valley already mentioned. It was the northern or Ganges valley Aryans who, in time, developed the law, custom, caste, as well as the modified religious system and the schools of philosophy, which we call "Hindu."[1] These ideas gradually spread (in after times) to the west and south of India—*i.e.*, to the Bombay "Dakhan" and to Madras, by the agency of Brahman missionaries. An Aryan (Yâdava) tribe, in a very early stage of development, came to the upper west, as has been stated; but into the upper part of Madras (Telingana) and the region farther south, Aryans never came, except in small numbers—Brahmans as teachers, and advisers to kings and princes, and soldiers of fortune seeking the command of armies, or posts of state.

Even in Northern India and the Indus valley the Aryan tribes (who were always engaged in wars which must have been a constant drain on their numerical strength) could not have formed a very large immigrant population. All the circumstances of their history indicate that they constituted a

[1] I may take it for granted that the reader is aware how the Hindu deities of the books called "Purâna" are entirely different from those that are found in the ancient Aryan Vedic Hymns.

limited and superior element, a ruling or dominant class, establishing kingdoms and providing territorial chiefs with their armies. They advanced, fully as much by alliances and the voluntary submission of the inhabitants, as by conquest. When the Aryans established their kingdoms in the Ganges valley, their armies and people generally (with the increase that certainly took place by the rapid growth of mixed and dependent races) could not have been maintained without a steady supply of grain, and without aid in building and other arts. This aid was, we must conclude, largely given by non-Aryan tribes. To be sure the Aryan races, or others originally associated with them, were not themselves ignorant of agriculture. Even in the hymns of the Rigveda, allusion is made to the measurement of fields, to corn and other agricultural produce; and the importance of the plough is sometimes recognised. And so it is in later literature. But agriculture was never esteemed by any, and was positively abhorred (as it is to this day) by the chief Aryan tribes—Brahmans and Warriors (Kshatriya). The "Vaiśya"—originally the bulk of Aryan "common people," and which Manu represents as the third *caste*, became to some extent an agricultural class,[1] and seem to have

[1] I need only say that the four castes—Brahman, Warrior (Kshatriya), commonalty or Vaiśya, and the added fourth caste or Śûdra, meaning mixed races, or strangers admitted into the Hindu pale—are rather terms of classification than actual caste names. Even Brahmans have to be described by a great

separated into two parts—one taking to trade, the other to cultivation. The poorer and non-combatant families would almost inevitably take to village cultivation in the course of time. It is impossible, however, on an examination of the existing agricultural castes (whether of tenants or owners) to trace the Aryan Vaiśya as having at any time formed any large element in the agricultural population.

It remains, then, briefly to note what became of the Aryan rulers, whose wars the great epic (the "Mahâbhârata") tells us of; and what other races come to Upper India. All we can gather is that the old Kshatriya kingdoms, one by one, disappeared,

number of local names; and instead of the "Vaiśya," we have a multitude of castes claiming respectable rank, though not of the warrior or priestly grade. The Śûdra represent all the converted races. The whole of the Hindu castes in South India (other than Brahmans) rank therefore as Śûdra. In a valuable paper (Dec., 1898) in the (Columbia) *Political Science Quarterly*, Mr. E. Washburn Hopkins, of Yale University, has recently given a number of references to Sanskrit literature bearing on villages and agriculture. He thinks I have allowed (in my "Ind. Vill. Comm.") too little of an agricultural character to the original Vaiśya. But my remarks were directed against the popular notion that the Vaiśya were an extensive and special caste *who introduced* agriculture into India. Some part of the common people of the Aryan group, it may be accepted, took to agriculture; but it can only have been a limited number. There is nothing whatever to shake my conviction that when the Aryans came it was as a superior, ruling element; that they found Dravidian (and Kolarian) tribes established; and that these tribes (or some of them) possessed irrigation "tanks," and had settled, organised villages. There is no kind of evidence that Aryans introduced agriculture, or that and that for a long period great parts of the Ganges valley were desolate; while in other parts, humbler mixed, or earlier non-Aryan races, resumed possession of the soil, and even produced chiefs and princes. Here and there, no doubt, Brahmanical and Buddhist kings continued to reign.

Meanwhile we have information that for a considerable period—say from 160 B.C. to 100 A.D., and again later on—there was a great disturbance of the Sakâ or "Indo-Scythian" and Yûchi or "Kushân" races beyond the west and north-west frontiers, and a consequent move forward (first of one, then of the other), which brought new elements into Indian

they invented any new village organisation. The whole mass of villages (as far as they are ancient) in the peninsula are of non-Aryan origin, since no considerable bodies of Aryans ever settled at all in those countries. And in Upper India, there is no indication that the mass of local agriculturists were connected with the Vaiśya, or more than partly Aryan at all. For when the superior Aryans ceased to rule throughout the great part of the Ganges valley, the country was re-occupied by Bhar, Pâsi, Chêru, and other agricultural tribes, who were certainly non-Aryan; whether any of them had been recognised by the Brahman classifiers as Śûdra is another matter. I will only add that I have never suggested that "India owes agriculture *and every settled principle of land tenure*" to the Dravidian races (Art. quoted, p. 677); but I am glad to take the opportunity of acknowledging that a sentence on p. 190 ("Ind. Vill. Comm.") is misleading. I meant only that non-Aryan races had established villages for agricultural life before the Aryans, and that the latter furnished the element of "overlordship" and manorial growth. This is not inconsistent with allowing that the lower ranks of Aryans, and especially the families of mixed blood, practised agriculture.

life in the north-west. We have to take account of the invasion of races who furnished the original materials of what are now the Jats, Gujars, and other similar tribes.[1] In process of time these tribes obtained settlements—especially in the plains of the Panjâb and adjacent parts of the N.W. Provinces—we can easily trace the area over which Jats, the prominent "community"-formers of the Panjâb,[2] and the Gujars, extended. At the same time, in place of the ruling "Hindu" race of the Kshatriya, we see the uprising of several notable tribes known as "Râjput," probably largely of Scythian or other foreign origin, and some of them descended from the old Aryan stock, but at most only semi-Aryan.[3] Some "Râjput"

[1] I state this generally; it is not meant that there were no other invasions which brought other tribes; or that we can be positive which tribe came in at which period. We know historically of one period of invasions in the time of Darius Hystaspes (sixth century B.C.); and the period spoken of in the text, which involved the loss of Greek rule in Upper India, the arrival of the kings known as the "Satraps," and then their displacement by the Kushân kings Kadphises, and (later) Kanishka, had the greatest importance of any.

[2] I may mention that in 1881—I have not the later figures at hand—Jats formed 195 *per mille* of the entire population of the Panjâb. Gujars are also very numerous. Both extended as far as Râjputâna.

[3] We feel sure of this on many grounds; but especially because a large number were grouped by the Brahmans (who directed religious and social life) into four great tribes or families called "Agnikula." These were said to have descended each from an ancestor who was miraculously born out of the sacrificial fire on Mt. Abu near Ajmêr. This means that their origin was

clans are traceable to an origin in Gujarât and Upper Western India, and others perhaps further north. It is certain that although the rule of Hindu or Buddhist kings never entirely ceased over Northern India, the local wars and foreign incursions gradually drove the Brahmanic or "Hindu" tribes towards the less fertile, but also more defensible, country of Râjputâna, Mâlwâ,[1] and Bundêlkhand—the tract roughly indicated as the country between the Jamna river and the Narbada. The first raids of the Moslem armies in mediæval times accentuated this tendency of the "Hindus" to congregate in this country. Doubtless during the whole of this period, the Jat and Gujar settlements in the Panjâb (and adjacent districts in the N.W. Provinces) were able to expand and to change considerably under the influence of the climate and of intermarriage. But when the Pathân emperors had established their rule, they began to employ and to encourage the "Râjput" chiefs, who were now thoroughly "Hindu." These often formed clans with a quasi-feudal order of organisation (wherever they were in sufficient numbers) and soon began to issue from Âjmêr, Mewâr, and the rest of Râjputâna, and

unknown (or not wished to be stated), but that they became Hindus by adoption, or at least espoused the cause of the Brahmans and their religion. We have no trace of the Râjput clans before the fifth century A.D.; indeed I might almost say before the eighth century.

[1] Mâlwâ is the country in Central India of which Ujjian was the well-known Hindu capital.

to re-possess the domains once ruled by Aryan princes in Oudh and the Ganges valley. This they did, sometimes under direct encouragement from the Moslem emperors, and often by mere adventure, in parts which had been left uninhabited, or were in the hands of tribes like the Bhar.[1] The important feature about the village communities in the N.W. PROVINCES and OUDH is this—that a very large number of them are Râjput villages, and they are almost, if not quite, invariably the result of this reflex movement, and *rarely, if ever, are older than mediæval times, i.e.*, from the date of the Pathân sovereigns of Delhi onwards. There are no traces of any certainly ancient Aryan village communities; and very few of clans or families having an ancient traditional connection with their present location, or said (with any probability) to be descended from the old Aryan races.

In the Panjâb (and in the parts of the N.W. Provinces more closely adjacent thereto) we have also some Râjput communities of a somewhat different origin;[2] but the great feature is the prevalence

[1] The traditional evidence, borne out by the facts of the case, appears in "Ind. Vill. Comm.," pp. 121-9 and 309 ff. Sometimes the Râjputs appear in clans, but without a monarchical constitution; in other cases single chiefs with a small following established "baronies" and small separate kingdoms in which there was no opportunity for a "feudal" distribution of territory.

[2] The Panjâb Râjputs are largely clans (Bhatti, etc.) descended (though probably in a much mixed race) from the original Yâdava tribes of the Indus valley and neighbourhood. In the parts of the Panjâb close to the N.W.P., some Râjputs are found of the same clans as those in the N.W.P.

of Jat, and (to a lesser degree) Gujar, villages. And, generally speaking, at the present day the tribal constitution of agrarian society is more prominent in the Panjâb than it is elsewhere. There are a number of other clans or castes of various names who have also joint-villages ; but they are either partly Jat or partly Râjput in origin, and may safely be classified with one or the other.[1] On the north-west frontier again there are settlements of tribes of quite special character. They are now (since some centuries) Moslem. These latter are very interesting, because we often possess almost complete information, not only about the whole tribe, but about the clans and sub-clans and ultimate divisions into which they are formed, and how they divided the land on which they settled (p. 24). And they retain various grades of chiefs who still exercise authority. But these settled at dates which (at the earliest) do not go back beyond five or six hundred years. They seem to have been, in their not very covetable territory (Peshâwar, Hazâra, Bannu, Kohât, Dera-Ismaîl *Kh*ân), left undisturbed by the greater sovereigns of the north, and probably professed a more or less nominal subjection to them. Whatever may be the reason, these tribes had not adopted a monarchical rule of their own ; and their "*Kh*âns," "Maliks," and other chiefs but rarely attempted to claim any extensive power or to attain large estates as local landlords.

[1] *i.e.*, referred to one or other of the northern invasions : such are the Ghakar, Awân, Arâîn, etc.

V

THE INDIAN VILLAGE AS IT IS

(*a*) *The Severalty* (*or* "*Raiyatwâri*") *Village*

THE preceding pages will have made it clear that all villages necessarily have certain features in common, but that as regards the ownership of the land within the group there is a broad distinction; and where this distinction exists, there is a concurrent difference in the village government (pp. 11, 12). In the "severalty" village the ownership is in the form of independent holdings, and there is no acceptance of a joint responsibility for the revenue and expenses; there is no joint ownership of the village site or of any adjacent waste area, and the village is found to be managed by a hereditary headman. Where the ownership is that of a joint body (in whatever shape), the co-sharers would never submit to the rule of one man, nor to an oligarchy of the chief and his deputies or other officers; they have (or once had) what I have called a standing council or committee of the (equal) heads of the co-sharing families to manage village affairs.[1] I have to give some account first of the "severalty" and then of the "joint" village, noting the races by which each kind was established, and describing the principle on which each appears to be constituted.

Of the severalty village there is, in the nature of things, only one form, and that form has been maintained in essential features, although in the oldest villages it is extremely probable that there has, in the course of time, been a loss of a certain tribal connection which once existed. The original villages were, as I have said, constituted at a time when the people lived in tribes and clans, so that the first organised villages were constituted by little sections of clans, each under its own leader or chief, who became the headman of the village. The land was distributed, according to custom, in lots to the several leading families and to the associate settlers. But as time went on, fresh villages would be started, not by considerable bodies of clansmen, but by numerous smaller offshoots from the villages first established. Small parties would go out (under a leader) and clear new plots in the jungle, and allot holdings among the settlers, so that the *form* of village was very like that of the original organisation

1 These heads constitute the *barâdarî*, or brotherhood proper. *All* the co-sharers and landowners are often described as *wârisân yak-jadi* = "heirs of the common descent." (This refers to the Panjâb.)

though there was no longer any question of tribal, custom in the establishment of new locations.[1]

Now, who were the people that first started organised villages in those countries where they are chiefly noticeable in the form we are considering?

We have seen that while Northern India is, as a matter of existing fact, covered with villages in the "joint" form, all India south of the Vindhyan hills—*i.e.*, all the central part of India, the Upper and Lower Dakhan, Madras, and Bombay (not to mention a great part of Bengal)—are entirely filled with severalty villages.

I think it is very likely that, at first, in Northern India also, villages were planted in this form, and that the Aryan domination, and afterwards that of later tribes of Râjputs, Jats, and Gujars produced the more compact or cohesive form instead. As far as Sanskrit authors (in Northern India) allude to villages, they either mention them without any specific mark indicating their internal constitution or else they indicate the severalty village under a headman.[2] And having regard to the fact that the

1 The same process has been going on ever since. In my 'L. S. B. I.," vol. ii., p. 451, I have given an extract explaining how villages were actually founded in the central regions of India; and it is extremely probable that exactly the same sort of thing has been always going on.

2 Mention of a village as a whole, or of the general boundaries of a village, does not imply that the whole was collectively owned, or that it constituted a "corporation." The boundaries of one village as against another are matters of the greatest im-

Aryans and other conquerors became monarchical, it is very likely that, apart from the chief princes and "barons" taking the rule over states and provinces,[1] cadets of the ruling families, courtiers, and others would soon obtain the lordship over individual villages, and become virtual owners of them, and so in time change the constitution in the manner which will presently be explained.

The villages as established by the humbler and purely agricultural tribes, whether Dravidian or Aryan, would be in the severalty form. All analogy of later times leads us to this inference. In the history of the mediæval Râjâs of Oudh, for example, it is clear that the subject villages were in the severalty form, paying the Râjâ's grain-share from each holding. And we have evidence how by grant (*birt*) of the king, or by the association of some local family, the village became owned by the joint heirs of such a grantee, and so acquired a different form.[2]

portance in village life, apart from any consideration of the village being jointly owned or otherwise. One of the most definite allusions to the village is in the "Laws of Manu," and there it is certainly the severalty village under a headman that is mentioned.

[1] I need hardly allude to the fact that in the Purânas and Epics the advance of Aryan tribes in the Ganges Valley is always represented under the guise of the great chief and his clan building a city and setting up a state of which it was the capital.

[2] This is very clearly brought out in Mr. W. C. Benett's admirable Settlement Report of the Gonda District in Oudh (1878). See §§ 64-77. The passage will well repay perusal.

It is really, however, unnecessary to pursue this question, as it is one on which there is, from the nature of the case, only "probable" evidence. Where we see the severalty village now, and also for centuries past, entirely occupying the country, is in the region of the Peninsula—beyond the Vindhyans. And it will at once strike us that to this part of India the Aryan invasion, and that of the later Indo-Scythian tribes, hardly extended at all. Circumstances evidently did not favour the development of lordships over villages, nor the constitution of bodies in a joint form. Joint villages did arise here and there, as we shall afterwards notice, but they were due to special causes. So, then, the severalty village is prevalent and characteristic in those very countries where the Dravidian element was strongest, and where it was least mixed with Aryan and later dominant races. This fact is entitled to weight as making it *à priori* likely that the prevalent village form is derived from institutions of Dravidian origin. At any rate, it seems manifestly impossible that the villages, as they exist, should be due to any Aryan invention or introduction. Now in the S.W. Bengal (Chota Nagpore) and in Orissa, we have some actual survivals which enable us to trace certain ancient undisturbed customs, which there is every reason to believe are those of the non-Aryan tribes, both Kolarian and Dravidian. In some of the more secluded districts we have distinct Kolarian races like the Santâl, Hô, Mundâ, etc.,[1] and also Dravidian, the Bhûiyâ, Kândh, etc.; and an apparently later tribe, the Urâon, who gave the name to Orissa, and furnished rulers over Chota Nagpore. And I do not think that anyone with local knowledge will be disposed to doubt that those peoples were organised in *tribes*, and that they established the territorial divisions still known as *nâd* (and by other names locally); and that the villages in these countries were, in the first instance, established by distributing or allotting the territory among the smaller groups, each led by its petty chief or chiefs, who in turn allotted the land within the village for the holdings of the various families or persons entitled to be provided for. I say in the first instance, because, as I have already remarked, as time went on new villages were constantly established one by one, by small groups starting out on their own account into the abundant waste, and clearing a new settlement, independently of the movement of a whole clan or sept, or other such body.

The Chota-Nagpore country, I should note, is admirably adapted to secure the preservation of old tribal forms of settlement, since it is fertile within and inaccessible to enemies from without, and does not lie in the track of any of the greater military movements known in history. Here we have distinct evidence that the Kolarian population was in part let

[1] "Ind. Vill. Comm.," p. 154 ff.

alone and in part combined with (or supplemented by) Dravidians, and all came under (later) Dravidian rulers. It is evident that the Kolarian settlements were, and still are, very rudimentary, and do not seem to have been likely to furnish a pattern to any more advanced tribes. The Kolarian tribes made small territories for tribal sections, locally known as *parhâ*. The boundaries were known, and each had a *totem* or distinctive emblem, which was (and still is) exhibited on a flag carried on festival occasions. Inside the *parhâ*, a few—I believe usually from ten to twelve—small and separate (family) groups of huts or cottages were built together. The people lived chiefly by herding goats and cattle, and by the chase; and what little cultivation was done was in a block adjacent to each hamlet. We are assured also by local observers that originally in the Kolarian hamlet the group was composed (like a "house communion") of a body of persons all descended from a common mother, and that the land such bodies cultivated was really held "in common," each block being in fact a plot sufficient to supply the needs of the group.[1] Apart from the fact that we have no evidence of any wide distribution of Kolarian races beyond the limits

[1] This question has been discussed by Mr. J. F. Hewitt in a paper in the Journal Roy. Asiatic Soc. for 1887 (pp. 628-641), and April, 1899 (pp. 329-356). It is not clear that the "common" cultivation went beyond the family hamlet, nor that all the land in the *parhâ* was held by the several sections in common; if, indeed, any definite ideas of property existed at all.

of the eastern districts of the upper peninsula and parts of the Vindhyan hills, it does not seem that this rudimentary form of village suggested to the later Dravidians *their* larger and better organised village, which we can also observe in the central Chota Nagpore districts. At any rate, it was such a *Dravidian village* that can be argued to be the direct progenitor of the surviving severalty form, whatever rudimentary form or forms may have a claim to be earlier still in point of time. Very good accounts of the organised villages are on record; and also a somewhat similar form is described among the Kândh tribe in Orissa.[1]

The important feature of these typical village settlements is that certain leading families of the group were the principal members (known as *bhûinhâr* families), and that other cultivators were associated with them, not necessarily, I believe, of the same clan. Out of these leading families were selected the headman (who also had one or more assistants or deputies), the *pahan* or priest, the *mahto* or "accountant." And allotments of land were made—one for the headman, one for the

[1] The village is described by Mr. Hewitt (who had been Commissioner and Settlement Officer both in Ch. Nagpore and in the Central Provinces), in Journal of the Soc. of Arts (May, 1887, p. 622). See also my "Ind. Vill. Com.," 179 ff., and Mr. Hewitt's paper on "Chota Nagpore" in the *Asiatic Quarterly Review*, April, 1887. The Kândh was a tribe which acknowledged marriage and the patriarchal family.

priest (and the maintenance of the deities), one for the *mahto*, and one for the other cultivators. Also a (fifth) lot was set apart to furnish grain for the support of the Râjâ, as tribal or local chief, which seems to have been the mode of raising a royal revenue even before the custom of taking a share in the grain from all the cultivators became general. As new cultivators joined the settlement, or fresh land was taken up, the whole of the holdings (perhaps with the exception of some of the privileged lots), were re-distributed or re-arranged. There was no appearance of the headman or of the privileged families owning the whole village (as superiors to the rest), or sharing it among themselves in fractions as joint-owners would do. The time came when the local chief (now Râjâ) was not content with the produce of the allotment of land in each village, but took a share in the grain of all the holdings except those of the privileged families; and this exemption may be suggested to have been the origin of the custom that the *pâtel* and *kulkarnî's* special holdings were in former days allowed to be free of State charges. (See pp. 10, 11.)

I have said that there is no appearance of such a constitution having any dependence on a "common holding," or of the settlers forming a body of owners in common. And though it is true that there were customs of periodically exchanging or re-distributing the holdings, I shall afterwards (in discussing the theory of primitive common holding) show that it affords no indication of an idea of "common property." The ruling idea was *allotment of a subsistence share in the tribal territory to every member*, according to his grade or position.[1]

It will be observed that in the severalty village, the nature of the *existing* constitution prevents there being any jointly-owned area of waste or grazing ground, or area available for eventual partition and extension of tillage. Each holding (in possession) is registered as the right of the person or persons cultivating it, and there is no scope for any joint-area. Nevertheless, where there is an adjacent area of waste, the village is allowed the use of it, though the land remains the property of the State. Whether, under such an organised tribal allotment of land as has been spoken of, each "village" was made definitely to include a tract of waste, I have seen no sufficient evi-

[1] Between the primitive villages of the Kolarians and the more perfect one organised with later Dravidian rule, there are naturally some stages of growth as well as local varieties ; but the principle is best exhibited in the Chota (or Chutiya) Nagpore villages. Mr. J. F. Hewitt has himself spoken of this principle—*i.e.*, the allotment of a subsistence holding to every member of the community—as comparable to that which Dr. Seebohm and his son have shown to have marked the old tribal life in Wales and in Greece. Mr. Hewitt, it is true, insists that the more perfect Dravidian (patriarchal) village, no less than the earlier (matriarchal) village, was "communal." But, in all his accounts, I have not succeeded in finding any mark of a "common holding," except the allotment and redistribution, which I cannot admit to be such.

dence. I think that it is highly improbable that any idea was entertained beyond the fact that a wide area (over which the villages were scattered) was *all*, in a general sense, the territory or heritage of the clan there located, and that each village might extend itself as it required. I can find no indication of any tribal custom of allotting a specific area of waste to each village—so much to this, so much to that, in the first instance. No doubt, in course of time, when villages became contiguous, the area of each would become definite. Should one village extend its cultivation so as to come into contact with the area which was habitually used by the next village, a definite boundary line would necessarily be arranged by the tribal authority. But we have no trace, that I can discover, of the ancient village being regarded (in each case) as owning a definite area of adjacent waste, *and* (as the necessary mark of such ownership) that this waste must (on partition being called for) be shared in the same proportions as the cultivated holdings. It seems more probable that, when the general tribal control of the whole area passed to a Râjâ, each village retained the right to the actually allotted lands in severalty, but that the waste was regarded as at the disposal of the Râjâ: though of course the king never thought of depriving a village of the use and enjoyment of the area which was, by custom, grazed over, nor would he object to their breaking up new pieces of waste when the village needed to extend its cultivation. It cannot fail to be observed that when the Râjâ made a grant of a "village," the grantee was always understood to have the right of improving the waste, though he would not have the right to oust the cultivators from their cultivated holdings. This seems to show that the right of the original villagers, beyond their cultivated holdings, was not a definite right of ownership, but a vague sort of user, though one limited to their own body.[1]

I shall not here pursue any argument that the existing form of severalty village is a real and independent form; and that if its derivation from the early form to which allusion has been made is not acceptable, then we must be content to say that its origin remains hidden, but that it certainly is not the result of any *decay* of such a form as we find in Northern India. That argument will come later. It will be observed that in those countries where the severalty village is prominent, it has been found necessary to adapt the revenue system to the tenure. Every holding is separately valued and assessed, and pays separately; no responsibility of one member for another is possible.[2] The revenue

[1] And a grantee, while cultivating the waste to his own profit, would still not attempt to do so to the extent of depriving the villagers of a sufficient area for grazing.

[2] The *raiyatwâri* method was essentially (*mutatis mutandis*) the ancient revenue system of the country, when the one-sixth (or other) share of the grain was taken from each holding in

system which treats the village as a *proprietary unit*, and lays one sum of revenue on it, is only applied to the "joint villages" of the North.

(*b*) *The Joint Village*

Just as the severalty village, with its headman and group of independent holdings, is characteristic of a great part of Bengal proper, of Madras and Bombay and Central India, so the joint village is found to be the prevalent form over the Panjâb, the N.W. Provinces and Oudh; and it seems probable that it extended over the adjoining districts of Bihâr (N.W. Bengal) at one time, only that the subsequent growth and acknowledgment of territorial landlords has almost obliterated the evidence.

each village. When, later on, the grain was converted into a cash-demand, or when the lump demand from a whole village was introduced, it was to save trouble in the collection, or to conceal an arbitrary increase. And when the collections began to be made in that way, it was everywhere necessary to introduce the "revenue farmer," or to make the village headman responsible, and arm him with arbitrary powers which first made it easy to depreciate and break down individual rights. Where there were "aristocratic" families or strong groups of clansmen, who could agree to the lump sum demanded, and be jointly responsible for it, there was the best chance of bearing up against official interference; but such a formation seems only to be possible under certain conditions. In modern times the system has wisely stereotyped the village unity only where it had naturally come to exist, as in North-Western India.

I have already intimated that these villages being "joint" are treated by the Revenue Administration as units; that the land within the boundary is either (in a few cases) held undivided by the co-sharing body, or it is divided into shares or lots separately enjoyed; but still the people do not object to be held "jointly and severally" liable for the revenue charge, local rates, and village expenses, the burden of which they distribute among the co-sharers according to the rule and principle of their constitution.

I have mentioned that the *existing* joint villages are not due to "Aryans," in the sense of any demonstrable connection with the old Aryan races. Some few communities may really be relics of old Aryan stock which escaped the destruction of the older wars; others may have a certain strain of Aryan blood but no more. In the main, it is true to say that while here and there some indefinitely ancient local tribes have joint villages, the formation of such villages in general is due to the later tribes—the Râjputs of various clans, the Jats and Gujars (p. 55 foll.), who are representatives of the various "Indo-Scythian" and other invasions of post-Aryan times.

To put it a little more explicitly, we may classify the villages according to race, as (1) Râjput settlers and adventurers (mostly mediæval) coming to Oudh, the N.W. Provinces and Panjâb, from an earlier home in Râjputâna, and other places; (2) Jat and Gujar communities largely found in the Panjâb, but extending into the parts of the N.W. Provinces more closely adjacent. The Jat class tends to run into the Râjput class very much; and it may well be that many in both ranks are of the same race, only that the more aristocratic and military were recognised by the popular custom as "Râjput," while the humbler and more purely agricultural were "Jat";[1] (3) a variety of other tribes, some earlier, some later, probably of mixed race, but approximating to (1) and (2); they are chiefly in the North Panjâb (Âwân, Ghakar, Arâin, etc.); (4) we may separate a group of (Moslem) tribes on the north-west frontier who are still living in a very perfect state of tribal organisation (p. 58); (5) in the S.E. Panjâb and elsewhere a number of villages have accepted the conditions of life under the joint village system, and yet are known to have started as associated colonists, forming village groups for defence and society, or otherwise to have been groups of independent holders, who, for one reason or another, have not objected to the joint constitution.

Next, as to the mode of formation, and the way in which the joint ownership arises. If we regard the whole mass of such villages, we shall observe that the principle on which the village body shares the land (waste and cultivated) within their boundary, is not

[1] This is all discussed and exemplified in "Ind. Vill. Comm.," pp. 99 and 277.

always the same. With the severalty village there is—perhaps can be—only one form. But here the joint-owners may share the estate, some in this way, some in that; or, in other words, the aggregate of co-owners may be formed on different principles or in different ways, so that there is more to be said about the joint village. And the first great distinction is that in *one* large class of villages the community (as a matter of fact) is a body descended from one man (or from one or two brothers) who obtained at some former time—maybe hardly a century ago, maybe six centuries or more—the lordship or superiority of the village. The "lord," however, in all cases, lived under what is the common rule not only of Hindus but of the landowning castes generally—the joint-family; this requires that when the head of the family dies all the male agnates who are heirs, according to their place in the table of descent, succeed together; so that in these cases it is really a (much expanded) family that has dominated the village and now constitutes the community.

In *another* class of cases the villages represent the fission of a whole clan or tribe; a large area is found entirely covered with cultivating, co-sharing groups of one and the same tribe, and governed by the same code of custom. Sometimes a number of villages are formed by the gradually multiplying descendants of a single original family or other small group settled on a wide space, which fortune preserved to it, till a number of village bodies grew up and separated off. Sometimes the village represents a body of sharers traditionally descended from one original founder, but not such a founder as pretended to any aristocratic rank (whose position the descendants continue to represent). They are merely equal owners of shares in the village; each head of a branch household possesses, and has always possessed, a divided share or lot. Sometimes the village owners have come together by voluntary association, and may or may not consist of families of the same clan or tribe. In all this large and varied class the shares or lots (however formed) are *not* according to the "ancestral" rule, as in the first class, and they have always been separately enjoyed from the first. As this second group itself requires sub-dividing, it will be better to explain the whole under *three* heads, which we will call—I. Ancestral; II. Tribal; III. Associate.

I. *Ancestral.*—The first class will be the form of joint village community just mentioned, in which the co-proprietary body is in fact a *dominant family* descended from one founder (or one or two related founders), who first obtained the superior position and took the "overlord's [1] share" of the grain from the village cultivators. As in the course of time they gradually multiplied, they came to form a co-

[1] To explain this word once more, I may refer to the note at p. 19.

sharing proprietary community of the village, numbering variously 30, 40, 60, or 100 members, or more, as the case may be. It is this kind of village that may sometimes exist in an *undivided* state; that is, the owners may never have divided the land at all, or may have never formally and finally divided it, but for the time each holds a certain portion, which (in theory) may at any time be recalled and adjusted, according to the "ancestral" share of each. In some cases part of the land is held divided, and part not. The undivided part is either the waste, grazing land, etc., which is more useful undivided, or is not yet required for the plough, and will be some day divided; or it is held by tenants, and the rents, not the land itself, are shared.[1]

In order to explain what is meant whenever the "fractional" or "ancestral" scheme of shares is referred to, let me explain that as primogeniture is never observed in peasant or village estates, the shares are the fractions of the whole which naturally follow from the principle of equal right in the same grade of descent or agnate male relationship, and are therefore fractions of the whole. Suppose, for ex-

[1] For the sake of Indian readers (others may pass it by), I mention that these conditions answer to the *zamindâri-khâlis* (the village lord is still a single individual); *zamindâri-mushtarka* (the joint family has succeeded, and the body have *not* partitioned); *pattidâri* (where the land *is* completely partitioned on the ancestral shares) and imperfect *pattidâri* (where the land is partly divided, partly not). In all these varieties the principle of sharing is one and the same: the *tenure* is not altered.

ample, that the original overlord leaves three sons; whether divided or not, there are three (major) shares (*pattí*). If one of those sons dies leaving two grandsons, the third share will be subdivided into two subshares (*thôk*); and if a grandson's share comes to be divided between, say, four great-grandsons (counting back to the founder), then we have four sub-subshares (*behri* or *tûla*), each consisting of one-fourth of one-half of one-third of the whole, and paying the corresponding fraction of the charges. Later descendant families will continue to succeed (within the major and minor groups to which they belong).[1]

[1] This diagram will at once explain how an ancestrally-shared (*pattidâri*) village is simply a continuation of a joint inheritance. I have supposed the whole village to consist of 2400 acres, and to have been founded by some distinguished person, and that the family are proud of this descent, and keep their share-scheme correct.

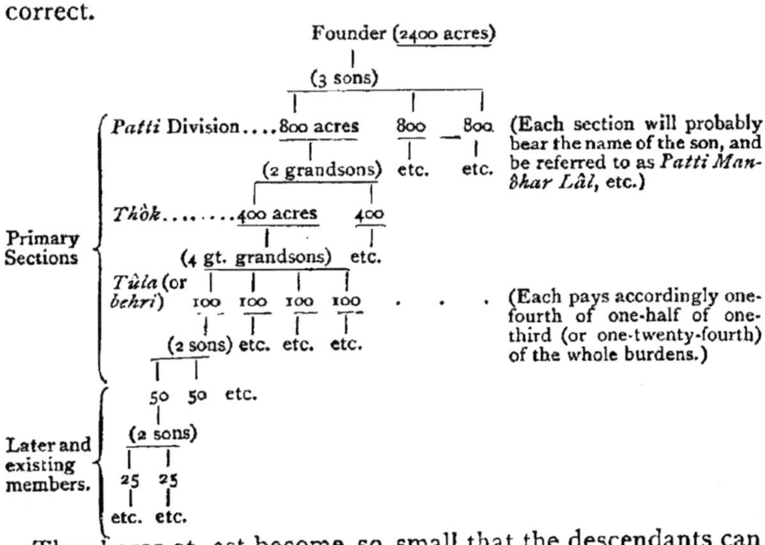

The shares at ast become so small that the descendants can

It will readily be understood that in paying the revenue and expenses, the fraction of the total sum (so long as the scheme is intact) corresponds with the fraction of the land owned.[1] But it often happens that in the course of time, owing to one accident or another, the shares cease to be exactly correct; and, especially if the case is one in which there has been no formal proceeding of partition, the holdings are likely to be irregular, and it is found impossible to remedy the variation (as will presently appear).

It sometimes happens that in a partly-divided village one part is correctly shared and the other not, *e.g.*, the cultivated holdings may be held according to existing "possession," but the waste (or other undivided) land may still be enjoyed (or its

no longer get a subsistence; but it will be remembered that very often a holder dies childless, and his share falls in to increase the holdings of the others, so that it may be long before an actual starvation limit is reached.

[1] The expenses being totalled, they are frequently spoken of in Indian fashion as one whole rupee, so that half the total is "8 anas," one-fourth is "4 anas," one-twelfth is = 1 ana 4 pai, etc. And to say that a man pays "four anas" revenue is the same as saying that he owns a four-ana share (or one-fourth) of the village. (I need hardly repeat the coinage scale, 1 rupee = 16 anas, 1 ana = 12 pai.) In the later stages of subdivision these divisions are not sufficient; and custom has provided a further scale, which is sometimes very curious, providing for a share which would be less than half an acre. See "Ind. Vill. Comm.," pp. 314-315, and note. In other cases the whole village is taken as one *bĭghâ* (area measure), and a half-share would be 10 *biswa*, etc.

income) in the correct ancestral shares, showing that the whole village was once governed by that rule and belonged to this class.'

As in *this* class of village it is possible that the estate may be actually undivided, it will be desirable to state the circumstances under which such a (rather exceptional) condition is maintained. It is well to take note of this with some care, because it is from such phenomena that the idea of "communal" ownership has emerged. I may mention also that in a few cases (under any class) plots of land may be found held undivided for some special convenience, and not connected with the custom of an undivided inheritance. In the case of a joint inheritance of the whole village, partition may have been put off owing to the jealousy of the heirs, who fear that one will get the better of the others; or it may be that the land is held by tenants, and that there is no object in dividing it, but a manager collects the rents and distributes the profits.[2] But what really happens in

[1] The varieties resulting from the shares becoming incorrect may be seen in detail in "Ind. Vill. Comm." p. 338. It is probably to distinguish such cases as those mentioned in the text that the official classification separates the "imperfect" (*i.e.*, partly divided) class of village.

[2] In every village, it will be understood, there may be the income from rents, and from wild produce, grass, grazing-dues, fruits, wood, etc., and perhaps small rents or dues from shopkeepers and occupiers of cottages in the village site. *Per contra*, there is the land-revenue, the local rates or cesses (for roads, schools, etc.), and the common expenses of the village, entertain-

most cases (though the village may still be formally recorded as "undivided") is that every co-sharer has taken possession of a certain farm, or some fields which he holds for his own benefit, the rest of the land (probably under tenants) and the uncultivated waste land is managed "in common," *i.e.*, the rents or profits from grass and wild produce are carried to meet the aggregate revenue charges and expenses of the whole body. If they do not cover it, the owners have to make up the balance according to their actual holding.

In the course of time such a state of things is very likely to become stereotyped. Each sharer is practically content with what he has got; or the weaker ones who have less than they ought see no chance of ousting the stronger; at any rate action is deferred till it is too late. In that case, the "ancestral share" scheme will have fallen into abeyance, and the *de facto* holdings (and proportionate payments) be recognised.

In a few cases, either by consent or in consequence of the form of association, special areas of land, perhaps unstable land, or land peculiarly situated with reference to moisture received by percolation from a river, will be cultivated without (permanent) division; strips or lots are marked out which are held

ing strangers, repairs to public buildings, etc., etc. When all are brought to account, the surplus is distributed in the proper shares.

in rotation.[1] This is the only exception. Ordinarily, any really "undivided" village will represent the estate of the joint descendants of one founder.

Such being the features of the tenure of this class of villages, it will be observed that it is *this* kind which we might well call "manorial," because, in fact, the village has been dominated by an "over-lord" (and his succeeding family), and has become a petty "manor." And although it is true that many such villages were newly founded in the virgin waste, by the aid of specially located tenants and dependents, still the position of the owner and his sons, as the superiors, is just the same, and they form the same major and minor divisions as the diagram has shown.

I need make no apology for repeating that this form of village really depends on the continuance (in an expanding circle) of the *joint-family* rule.[2] More need not here be said; but I shall have some

1 See "Ind. Vill. Comm.," p. 281, and in my "L. S. B. I.," Vol. II., pp. 142, 640, there is a diagram illustrating the method of division and the reasons of it.

2 Sir H. S. Maine has justly observed that the joint family is not the same as the village community; but in the class of cases we are considering the latter arises out of the former simply by continuing the division and re-division of the shares, as far as the limits of the village and the possible smallness of a holding will admit. It is a group of families, themselves all subdivisions of one larger family. Of course in the large class of joint villages constituted by clans or by associate groups, the "joint family" idea has little or nothing to do with the union.

further observations to make in a closing section which relates to ideas of property in land.

It may be observed that this form of village with its major and minor divisions (*pattî*, *thôk*, etc.) is the automatic result of the growth of a family and of the partition of the land (see diagram, p. 77). It is not an organisation designed or pre-conceived ; and most probably when the "founder" of the village began his career, his first thought was not to dispossess the older cultivators or overshadow the headman, or consciously to introduce a new form of tenure, but merely to take the "lord's share" of the produce, and to cultivate, for his own benefit, what land he chose, which was not already under the plough. But such a position was sure to develop into a virtual ownership, as it has in any case of "landlord" tenure in India, whether the superior's title is over one village, or two, or a hundred. And when the "founder" was succeeded by his joint heirs, the village "owners" became a community. I will further add that in this class of cases the proprietary family are very often of Râjput or some other superior (or at least non-cultivating) class, and that they almost always have *tenants* under them. Sometimes the poverty of the family may have compelled them to work their own lands, with the aid of the village menials at sowing time and harvest. It will be well to give some idea of the circumstances under which such a domination of villages has taken place

—how such families came to have the pre-eminence.

(1) A very common case (and one of the *latest* origin in point of date) is where a revenue-farmer has grown into proprietor. He undertook to be responsible personally for the whole sum assessed on the village, and what with taking over the lands of persons who failed to pay, and by means of mortgages and purchases of this field and that, the "farmer" became, in time, "owner" of the whole village. And be it recollected that at the beginning of the nineteenth century, before the idea of a single landlord was abandoned, managers of villages, principal sharers, and others, were constantly treated as sole proprietors, and their families have actually expanded into dominant co-sharing communities. This was not always attended with injustice; such persons (having a little capital) often took charge of abandoned villages and restored the cultivation by their own means; or they became responsible for cultivating groups too dispirited and poverty-stricken (*e.g.*, after the Rohilla troubles) to claim any independent rights.[1]

(2) A large number of villages (often of Râjput or other higher caste) derive their proprietary communities from an ancestor who had received a grant of the village from the ruler, the grantee being thus rewarded for military or other service, or getting it as a means of support.[2]

(3) Similar "rights" were obtained by some energetic family settled in the place; their growth being due to their superior wealth, energy, or influence.[3] In all these cases, observe that the original grant or usurpation was not formally of the ownership, nor did an usurping resident think at first of ownership. It was the "king's share," or perquisites of authority, that were

[1] See "Ind. Vill. Comm.," p. 303, and the references there given. In the Bareli district (N.W.P.) out of 3,326 villages, 2,611 had become the property of dominant families in this way.

[2] See *Id.*, p. 301. Brahman or (Moslem) Saiyad families constantly own villages formed in this way—the village having been granted as a work of religious merit.

[3] *Id.*, p. 310 ff., and p. 321.

granted, or an "overlord" share of the produce that was demanded from the cultivators, as the case might be; this was understood to include the right of improvement of the village waste land; and so the dominant right grew into a virtual proprietorship as I have said; the older inhabitants (if there were any) frankly accepting the position of tenants.

(4) But a more curious mode of growth of "manorial" joint-bodies occurs, when it is not the single village as such that has been the subject of a grant, but a larger area has become the scene of the domination or territorial rule usually of some Râjput Râjâ, or perhaps a Moslem chief, with his family and followers. In such a territory there were sometimes separate portions which had been made over as the "fiefs" of some of the Râjâ's principal male relatives. At first this was all a question of rulership, or the exercise of "baronial" jurisdiction, taking a share of the produce from the cultivating bodies already established, and founding new villages in the waste by inviting tenants and dependants and offering them a settlement. Then (in time) in village after village the ruler's rights and perquistes, were alienated or made over, one by one, as appanages or as life-grants for the support of cadets and scions of the family. In time the descendants of such grantees become the co-sharing owners of the whole group of different villages. Very often, too, a petty barony or territorial estate, such as we are speaking of, never adopted any rule of primogeniture, and became formally partitioned (on the occasion of a succession) village by village; thus each relation getting a village stood in the place of founder or ancestor, and his descendants form the "community."[1] Sometimes misfortune overtook the rulership; the principal members followed the Râjâ to battle, and were dispersed or slain; then such of the descendants as survived clung to a village here and a village there, while the conqueror took possession of the territory.[2] The whole former "barony"

[1] Instances of this may be seen in "Ind. Vill. Comm.," 308 ff. See especially the case of the (Râjput) Gautam Clan of Argal, p. 312.

[2] As to the village proprietary body arising on dismemberment

(or the *râj*) then became a district of the Empire, but was covered by villages, often held by bodies of descendants of the former ruling house.

It is in connection with *these* modes of the growth of communities of co-proprietors over the villages that I have to mention a feature which is conclusive as to the character of the process. There are cases in which the "proprietary communities" *do not correspond to the several geographical villages* as they stand; but the co-sharing bodies correspond each to a certain "estate" or group of lands (*mahâl*)[1] arranged by their family division; some land lying in one village, some in another; and the entire group of holdings which belongs confessedly to one "house," to the descendants of one man (who have to be assessed together in one sum), has to be represented on paper by bringing together in a list, the several lots.

These features are more particularly noticeable in the N.W. Provinces and Oudh among the higher caste village communities; but there are also cases in the Panjâb; and it is highly probable that something of the kind occurred in the Bombay or Dakhan villages when they became held (in former days) by *mirâsdâr* families; only that in this latter case the overlord families died out (*see* Appendix).

II. *Tribal.*—The next class of village is also marked by the cohesion of the landholding co-sharers, who combine to accept a joint responsibility (at least do not object to it), and readily accept the joint-ownership of such area of waste as is included

of ruling families and their territory, see "Ind. Vill. Comm.," pp. 308 ff., specially p. 314.

[1] Which becomes the unit with which the Government deals. A notable instance of this occurs in the Azamgarh district (N.W. Prov.).

in the boundary of their village at survey. And when this land is partitioned—being wanted for extension of cultivation for the increasing members—it will be divided out on just the same proportions as those in which the older cultivated land is held[1] But here we do *not* observe that the village is divided into fractional (ancestral) shares, because the villagers, though possibly of common descent, are not representative descendants of an overlord; and the class I have here separately distinguished is, in fact, either derived from a tribe (or smaller "clan") settling on a sufficient area, and dividing the whole out into shares—so much land for each person or each head of a house, or else the villages originated in one centre, where a small group of settlers found a home on a wide space, which fortune has preserved to it. In the course of time the families have multiplied and filled the whole area, and the separating groups have formed so many "villages" which at first were acknowledged as dependent on the parent centre, but in time became completely independent groups, each with its own establishment, its own assessment as a unit, and so forth.

It is often that we observe quite a large area now covered by villages all of the same caste or tribe, and they believe rather mistily in a common descent; but

[1] If a man owns land which is one-twentieth of the area of the arable, he will also receive one-twentieth of the waste area when it is partitioned.

they cannot always say whether their predecessors came there *as a body* already existing, or whether only a few men settled, and have, in the course of two centuries or more, gradually grown into the existing number.[1] In these cases the tribe or group are sometimes spoken of as constituted "democratically" —*i.e.*, there was no Râjâ or baronial government, and, as a rule, no dominant families to take possession of this or that village. In many of these cases the village shares represent an allotment made by the tribal chief of an (equal) share to every member of the clan or group settling there, or they are merely the holdings which the growing households have added on, one by one, out of the abundant area, without any formal process of division at all. This class of village is more especially common in the Panjâb, but is by no means unknown in the N.W. Provinces and Oudh.

Under this class the most striking illustration is afforded by the north-western frontier clans, who are so comparatively recently settled (from two to six hun-

[1] For examples, see "Ind. Vill. Comm.," p. 266 ff., especially pp. 276, 282. In some cases, the (large) area will be found to be divided on the ancestral principle, as far as the first or principal sections—*i.e.*, the shares of the *original* sons of the family, and *their* sons and grandsons. That is because while the number is very small and the area large, it is easiest to make the allotment so. But afterwards, all the new descendants take equally; their lots are compared and valued in a peculiar way, so that the share of payment is in just correspondence with the extent and value of the holding.

dred years ago) that their constitution is well known, and the distribution of their land in sections and sub-sections is plainly visible on the ground (p. 24); while the tradition of the chief, and how he made the distribution of lots—first the major territories and then the final groups—is still well preserved.[1] This distinct evidence is peculiar to the frontier districts; but it will be observed that very much the same thing most probably occurred when the Jat and Gujàr tribes settled down in the more central plains, and we have many instances in which the exact rule or principle of their sharing is not now remembered.

It is not at all necessary that the shares or lots should all be made by nearly equal measures of land. That would not suit if the territory were very various in quality of soil or in advantages of irrigation. I must not go into details of each mode of distribution which is followed *both* in this and in the next (III.) class. One method, however, is curious: it consists in making the holdings consist of certain measures, which, though called *bîghâ*, are not the standard land measure, but artificial lots made up of little bits—usually long strips—of as many different kinds of soil as there are in the settlement.[2] Where so much

[1] For details, see my "Ind. Vill. Comm.," pp. 247 and 253.

[2] For a singularly perfect example among Jats in the Mathura district (N.W.P.), see "Ind. Vill. Comm.," p. 283. This is what is properly meant by the term *bhaiâchârâ*. The artificial measures are spoken of as *bhaiwâdi-bîgha*, *tauzî-bîghâ*, etc. The

elaboration is not needed, the object of making the burden (of taxes, etc.) is equal attained by counting the *bíghá* of poor land as twice or thrice as large as the *bíghá* of rich.

It is very common in this class of village to find the holders of shares cultivating their own lands, though tenants may also be employed.

One other special feature may be added. Cases are observed in which (in this class) there were originally no "villages" at all to begin with. The whole area was divided out once (or gradually as required) into lots for all the tribesmen. For instance, on the north-western frontier, the land for the ultimate section or "company" (called *Khel*) often formed an area far larger than the usual "village" (pp. 8, 25). In other places also, the whole of a large area is known to have been divided into shares for the households without definite village groups.[1] But as time goes on, and families of the same connection multiply, and their cultivation is more or less aggregated in blocks, the area becomes divided up into villages, for convenience of survey and for other administrative reasons. Moreover, as the cultivation extends, the connected families belonging to one stock set up their cottages in one hamlet, which soon becomes large

bíghá, as an ordinary area measure in use in India, varies in different provinces. Commonly, it is five-eighths of an acre.

[1] For examples, see "Ind. Vill. Comm.," pp. 270-271, and also at pp. 262, 285, and as to the larger (frontier) *Khel* areas splitting up into villages, see *id.*, pp. 245, 251, 261, etc.

enough to require a separate staff of artisans, etc., and a separate mosque or shrine.

It is curious to observe that among tribes which, like the Jat, are, as a rule, agricultural and "democratic," *some* of the villages are found to have been dominated by single families, and to be held on the ancestral (*pattidâri*) scheme. This shows that here and there a particular chief, or his son, or some leading person, has managed to get possession of a village, and made it his "manor."[1]

It is a fact, of which I have seen no satisfactory explanation, that some tribes have never developed the monarchical (quasi-feudal) form, under which the clan and sectional chiefs become "Râjâ" and "barons," and establish a military and territorial rule. Even among the Râjput tribes, where this system was often so fully developed, and is described in Colonel Tod's "Rajasthan" with so much animation, we observe *some* clans who never had Râjâs,[2] but merely acknowledged the "patriarchal" authority of their sectional chiefs, and formed villages, or groups of tribal families holding land in allotted shares, on a

[1] It would be very interesting, if our statistical information were such as to show (for the Panjâb), how many of the entire mass of the Jat villages are held on the ancestral or *pattidâri* plan. It is at present uncertain how far the early Jat races had Râjâs and a monarchical rule like the "Hindus."

[2] Those who care to pursue the subject will find some excellent remarks in the *Oudh Gazetteer*, Vol. II., p. 40 (Article Hardoi).

general principle of equality. In the interesting province of Benares, where a "landlord settlement" was made according to the ideas of those days (1795), but where, properly speaking, the joint villages should have been dealt with as such, it is noticeable that the (Râjput) clans often adopted the (non-aristocratic) tribal allotment plan, and had artificial lots or land-measures, so as to make the advantages and the burdens of land-sharing as equal as possible.[1]

It will be asked: If this method of alloting equal shares (in one form or another) to all the members for their several enjoyment is *the* feature of so large a class of village, where does the *joint* property come in? It is really rather a matter of natural union caused by the sense of common descent or common tribe, and, in consequence, the observance of tribal custom of pre-emption, and of a rule against alienating land outside the agnatic group, or to the prejudice of natural heirs. To this we must add the knowledge that by becoming mutually responsible and acting together, the whole village could best be preserved both from outside enemies and from the disintegrating effects of a harsh and exacting government;—when a revenue-farmer is kept at a distance,

1 And this feature sorely puzzled the Resident (Mr. Duncan) in 1796, when he reported on the villages, and noticed the *bhaiwâdi bîghâ*, or artificial measures, which he attributes to quite a wrong cause. This curious report is, I believe, the first in which "joint" villages came to notice, and it ought to be reprinted.

by the united body offering to pay a lump sum for the whole village, and being jointly answerable for its being forthcoming at due date. Moreover, such a combination involves the joint ownership of the village site and the wells, etc., within the boundary, which, from the nature of the case, cannot be partitioned, and also the joint ownership of the grazing land or other waste not yet divided.

It will be asked also: How is it that a "tribal allotment" in Central and Southern India is argued to have been the origin of the separate shares in the severalty village, while apparently a closely similar arrangement in the north country resulted in the united community villages?

It seems to me that as the Dakhan (or peninsular) village must have received its primary form centuries before these northern groups came into existence, there has been more time for the sense of tribal union to wear out;[1] also that very likely there was not the same necessity for combination against enemies, or perhaps not the same character or cohesiveness. But, as regards the north-west frontier villages, they really *are* very much like severalty villages, except that the tribal union is strong, and the custom of not alienating land to the prejudice of heirs survived, and that the democratic character of the tribes does not allow the sectional chief or headman to have so much direct managing authority.

[1] This matter will come up again in another connection.

Indeed, it must always be remembered that the frontier villages (and the same is true of the clan areas in the Salt Range country or Jihlam district of the Panjâb) are not really at all like the kind of joint village which the N.W. Province system first adapted itself to; they have little in common with the *pattidâri*, etc., of the text-books; only that, having certain features of union, they naturally suited the system which was applied to them, and so the villages have become classified in the statistical records as of the same nature as the others.

III. *Associate.*—The third class of village—still one that has features which enable it to be managed on the "joint" principle—is rather a residuary one; nor is it easy to draw a sharp line between it and the class II. There is the same absence of the "ancestral share" system, *i.e.*, there is no appearance of the village having been dominated or founded by one man, whose descendants the present superior community or brotherhood represent. The shares are either equal lots—where the soil is fairly uniform—or they are arranged on the method of making each holding consist of strips of good, bad, and indifferent land together; or the holdings are adapted to the "ploughs"—the number possessed by each cultivating household. Or perhaps the village is an irrigated one; wells have been sunk at suitable distances, and the land is shared with reference to the proportion of labour and money which each village co-proprietor contributed to the (co-operative) well sinking.

(1) In these villages we sometimes see different sections (*tarf*) occupied by families of a different origin, whose tradition is that they clubbed together and got lands together in one circle for defence.[1] A still more interesting example occurs among various clans of Jats, who settled—on being compelled to move from some earlier locations—in the eastern part of the Panjâb.[2] The villages not only belong each to a separate clan or sub-division of Jats, but *inside* each village will be found "sections," each held by families of a different clan, who have clubbed together for defence. Near the same locality may also be found (in interesting contrast) large areas entirely occupied by villages all of one clan. The land is here (inside each village) divided out into so many *hal* or "plough lands," a number being assigned to each family in proportion to its strength. And very often (where the soils differ much in value) the lots are made up of specimen strips of each kind.

(2) Another kind of village—notably in the S.E. Panjâb—is known by uniform tradition to have been formed, at no very distant date, by voluntarily associated parties of colonists, each under a leader.

[1] See the example (Gujrât district, Panjâb) in "Ind. Vill. Comm.," p. 339.

[2] In the Lûdiâna district there is a very full account of these curious settlements, which I have abstracted in "Ind. Vill. Comm.," pp. 274-6.

Here land-shares were at once made out, and were distributed among the cultivating families by the process of casting lots.[1] Here there was nothing to distinguish the village from the severalty form, except the willingness of the people to accept a joint responsibility for the revenue. They did not settle under any special grant of privileged tenure as in the (quite exceptional) case of the Madras colonists noted in Appendix I. But the villagers had no objection to come under the "joint" system of the N.W. Provinces, and gladly accepted the recognition of their joint ownership of such areas of adjacent waste as the survey proceedings adjudged to be included in their boundary, and to form part of the joint village estate.

It will be observed that in all these cases the origin of the village is known—all the facts tend to confirm the tradition of origin. There are, of course, many other villages in which the proprietors—each in possession of a certain lot of land which he cultivates separately—have no recollection of their origin, nor of how they came by their "*de facto* possession." All they can say is, that the land share is the "gift of Providence," or that they have always cultivated

[1] See "Ind. Vill. Comm.," p. 323 ff. As to the temptation or opportunity for the leader of such a party to erect himself into a petty landlord, and the instructiveness of this, as illustrating the way in which a dominant body may grow up in a village of any kind, see my "L. S. B. I.," ii., p. 691, and the quaint verse quoted in the footnote.

"according to their ability." They *may* have once had some definite system of sharing, as in class I. or II., but they have forgotten all about it.[1]

And, lastly, it has to be noted that in some cases, villages like those in Kângra (Panjâb Hills) in Ajmêr, and in Jhânsi (N.W. Provinces bordering on Central India) are only artificially introduced into the class of joint villages; and that in some cases trouble has resulted. In the S.W. Panjâb, too, there are no real villages: separate farms or holdings have been clubbed together with the intervening waste, and *made* into villages.[2]

A more curious instance still is afforded by the *Central Provinces*, which (under circumstances detailed in my "L. S. B. I." Vol. II.) it was determined to settle (for the most part) under the N.W. Provinces system. As the villages were, really and naturally, severalty villages, and the circumstances of the inhabitants such that they could not accept the joint responsibility, and did not care to have an area of waste made over (as a

[1] Hence in the returns, all are, or were, lumped together as *bhaiâchârâ* villages—estates held "by custom,"—quite forgetting that the real tenure so called was a definite and original custom, and that, from the tenure-student's point of view, the mixing up of all these villages in one undistinguishable mass is most unfortunate. We shall see afterwards how one theory of "evolution" has been grounded on this confusion.

[2] In Ajmêr at the latest Revenue Settlement, the joint responsibility was virtually abolished. As to the troubles in the case of the Jhânsi districts, see "L. S. B. I.," Vol. II., pp. 120-1. As to the (Multân and other south-western) Panjâb holdings, see "Ind. Vill. Comm.," p. 65.

joint property) to each body, the Government determined to *confer* the proprietary right on the headman or on the person whom the Mahrâthas had made answerable for the revenue (our officers called him the *Mâlguzâr*). And so the original villagers became "sub-proprietors," or tenants with occupancy rights, according to circumstances. In course of time the sons and families of the grantee-proprietors will form "joint communities" owning the villages.[1]

[1] Those who are curious to follow the history of the experiment will find it described in "L. S. B.I .," Vol. II., pp. 382-385.

VI

THE THEORY REGARDING INDIAN VILLAGES EXAMINED

HAVING sketched the main facts about Indian villages, it is now time to consider the theory to which I have alluded, and to inquire how far it corresponds to the reality of things. As we have been led to establish the clear distinction that exists, *ab origine*, between the "severalty" and the "joint" forms of village, so an examination of the theory must be divided into two portions. I proceed to show (*a*) that the theory fails altogether to apply to the severalty village of peninsular India; and (*b*) that it fails to account satisfactorily for even the limited class of joint villages found in Northern India, on which (in reality) it is based. In order that the theory itself may not be misrepresented, let me set down its distinctive features *seriatim* and give the appropriate references. The theory is that:

(1) The Indian village communities may differ locally and in detail; they may exhibit signs of decay and change; but for purposes of comparative study

they may be represented by a single typical form to which all approximate.[1]

(2) The essential feature is that the village land is owned "in common" (or "collectively"); and that even where allotment in severalty has taken place, the idea of "cultivation in common" is kept up by minute rules regulating the tillage of the several holdings.[2] The typical village has no headman, or single chief, being governed by a committee or council of the brotherhood.[3]

(3) Sir H. S. Maine speaks of the typical village

[1] "V. C.," p. 107: "I am attempting to describe a typical form to which the village communities appear to me on the evidence I have seen to approximate, rather than a model to which all existing groups called by the name can be exactly fitted."

[2] "V. C." p. 41: "The system is one of *common enjoyment* by village communities, and inside those communities by families." Again (p. 107): "The common life of the group or community has been so far broken up as to admit of private property in cultivated land, *not so far as to allow departure from a joint system of cultivating* . . ." And "minute" or "multifarious" rules are spoken of as enforced with the object " . . . to *reconcile a common plan and order of cultivation on the part of the whole brotherhood* with the holding of distinct lots . . . by separate families." And (p. 222) "joint ownership by bodies of men was the rule . . . several ownership by individuals the exception." See also (p. 227): "Ownership *in common* by large groups of men originally kinsmen." (The italics are mine.)

[3] "V. C.," p. 123: " . . . in those parts of India in which the village community is most perfect . . . the authority exercised elsewhere by the headman is lodged with the village council" (*cp. id.*, p. 155).

marked by collective ownership, as archaic and representing the universal primitive idea of property. Further, that it was the creation of the Aryan races (*i.e.*, in India, the Sanskrit speaking tribes of the Vedic and Epic Poems).[1]

(4) Originally the bodies owning in "common" had no definite shares; the acknowledgment of them (in one form or another) was a later invention—a stage in the process of development from "common" to "individual" property.[2]

[1] This appears *passim*. See for instance "V. C.," p. 220 and "E. H. I.," p. 77, where the admission that the village community is *now* known outside the Aryan limit, implies the Aryan origin as regards India. The question of any kind of village in India being Aryan or not might be regarded as an ethnological problem of no great practical importance. But in fact it is made use of to confirm the idea of general primitive common ownership, because the Indian village is thus linked on to the (supposed) "Teutonic mark," which is itself Indo-germanic or Aryan. Moreover, Sir H. S. Maine shared the belief (see "V. C.," p. 104) which has been repeated from book to book without verification, that the "Law of Manu" contains allusion to the *collectively owned* village; this, however, is not the case. The village of separate holdings under its headman is certainly the only kind of village referred to by Manu—or (to the best of my belief) by any other early Sanskrit writer (but see p. 61.)

[2] The passage "V. C.," p. 81, no doubt refers directly to the "Teutonic mark"; but the whole drift of the remarks is, I think, that *shares* in the village do not belong to the real original form. *Cfr.* "E. H. I." pp. 79-81, where the Hindu joint family is referred to. (In the judgment there referred to, Lord Westbury did not mean that no member has a definite share [dependent on his place in the table of descent] which he certainly has, but that no particular plot of land, or piece of

(5) The groups consist of persons originally connected by consanguinity, or at least assumed to be so; this was in time more or less completely forgotten, and the body is now held together solely by the land which the members cultivate in common.[1] The (only) *raison d'être* of these communities is the tillage of the soil.[2]

(6) And lastly, we are informed that these communities are not simple bodies, with equal rights: they are composite groups, containing social layers amalgamated at different (remote) times; so that the whole composes a sort of hierarchy from the highest caste down to the lower artisans, labourers, etc.[3]

property represented the "share" of any member before partition.)

[1] "V. C.," p. 175: "At the outset they seem to be associations of kinsmen united by the assumption (doubtless very vaguely conceived) of a common lineage." "E. H. I.," p. 78: "cultivating groups . . . in which . . . the assemblage of cultivators is held together solely by the land which they till in common." And compare *id.*, p. 81.

[2] "V. C.," p. 175: "The end for which it exists is the tilling of the soil." Sir H. S. Maine seems to have forgotten that in fact (especially in the North-West Provinces) a large number of the communities were of non-agricultural, commercial, or military castes, and that Râjputs, in particular (unless reduced by poverty), never cultivated; their *raison d'être* was not tillage; they looked to the land as a source of livelihood from rents paid to them as "lords of the manor."

[3] "V. C.," p. 117: "Various subordinate groups which it may be shown to include." *Id.*, p. 123: "Not simple, but composite bodies, including a number of classes with very various rights and claims." And especially p. 175: "*The brotherhood*" (italics are mine), "*besides the cultivating families* who form the major

(*a*) *The Theory with reference to the Severalty* (*or Raiyatwâri*) *Village—the more widespread form*

It is obvious that the village in which there is a hereditary headman, and a number of holdings which never were joint or "in common" at any known historic period, does not, as it stands, in any way whatever correspond to the typical form with the six characteristic features just enumerated. That, however, is not denied by anyone who supports the theory of original unity. Their line of explanation is, first, very much to underrate the importance and the widespread and regular prevalence of this form of village, and the distinctive character of the features by which it is marked; next, to rely on the existence of features which *all* villages must, as I have insisted,[1] alike possess, as suggesting that all were originally of one type; and thence to conclude that the severalty villages were once held in common, and that they "decayed" into the existing form; that they "passed under" the government of a single headman, who was believed to have replaced (perhaps by the action of the Government of the time), an earlier "council of elders." An examination of the question indicated by the heading, then, resolves itself into a considera-

part of the group, *comprises families* hereditarily engaged in the humble arts which furnish the little society. . . . *It includes* a village watch and a village police. . . ."

[1] p. 14.

tion of how these severalty villages really came to be so widespread; whether or no there was, or could have been, the decay or change spoken of; and lastly, to examine certain local facts which (being misunderstood) have served to support the decay theory by showing the existence at some former time of joint villages in the south of India.

I have already (p. 63 foll.) given some details showing the probability that the severalty village is a direct derivation from a Dravidian form, of which the important feature is that the holdings were all *allotted*, and separated according to fixed custom, for enjoyment of the different persons and classes entitled, from the first establishment of the village. There is no appearance of a common ownership, or that the several families, whether specially privileged or not, ever regarded themselves as a joint or co-sharing body. Nothing of the kind has been established. Where we find traces of former *shares* (of a joint holding) in villages in certain parts of the Dakhan, these occur under circumstances that show them to be special growths, and emphasise the contrast between them and the ordinary conditions of village constitution. The severalty village, as it has already been described, would very naturally arise out of such a (Dravidian) form as we have considered. In the course of centuries, the once existing tribal connection, and the feeling of clanship, would gradually die out, and the allotted holdings would cease to be exchanged or re-distributed—would become held by persons of different origin, and so become wholly independent (as holdings), although the village might retain its headman and such a distinctive feature as his (free) *ex officio* holding of land in the village, and the habit of reliance on the headman's authority and help. That, by a process of decay or transformation, it should have *taken on* these peculiar features; or, in other words, that these should have become substituted for a once common or collective ownership and a joint management carried on by a council or committee, as the theory is, seems to me in the last degree incredible.

It may, indeed, be objected: "You attribute the separate and independent holdings in this kind of village to an *original* distribution of appropriate lots to each free member of the village group, which was probably the section of a larger clan; does not the existence of this widespread, customary rule that every tribesman is entitled to a lot or share in the acquisition of the clan or tribe imply an antecedent idea of 'community' of property?" It has been held that it does, but chiefly, it would appear, because of a custom of periodical re-distribution or exchange of holdings which is observed among several tribes. In the north-west frontier tribal villages,[1] re-distri-

[1] These are specially instanced, though of very much later origin and somewhat different form, because the allotment of holdings on the settlement of the tribe is an undoubted fact, of

bution (*vêsh*) undoubtedly prevailed—in some cases till quite recent times. But when permanent occupation and labour bestowed begin to tell, it is gradually given up; and when the holdings were embanked or terraced by special effort or labour and expense the custom did not apply at all. I regard this customary re-distribution as a symbol, not of "common" property, but of equal individual right; it prevents one man from permanently securing a more valuable share than his fellows. Equality in the value of holdings is much thought of in view of individual, separate right; it would have no meaning if the land was held "in common" and cultivated for the benefit of a common

which there is clear evidence, as there is also of the periodical exchange and re-allotment of the holdings. But there are also indications that in the Dravidian village the holdings were liable to re-arrangement when fresh waste was taken up and the number of ordinary holdings was to be increased. Traces of re-distributive custom in the Chhatîsgarh district (Central Provinces) and South Arcot, in Madras, are sometimes appealed to; but the latter are quite modern, and were arranged with a view to facilitate the payment of the revenue charge. And in Chhatîsgarh the cases *may* have been connected with some remembrance of an earlier *custom;* but the reported instances of actual exchange date from Mahrâtha times, and were connected with the cultivating arrangements made (or rather, I should say enforced) by the Revenue Manager. I do not, however, lay any stress on this, because, as explained in the text, voluntary exchange or re-distribution certainly was, in some cases, a regular feature of the "tribal allotment" system. See "Ind. Vill. Comm." pp. 256-7-9, and "L. S. B. I.," vol. II., pp. 377-8.

fund: then it could not matter whether one holding was more or less productive than another, or who cultivated the best land. At any rate there is no necessary connection between such a custom and a common holding; and before accepting such a connection, one would like to ask whether any vestige of a case is known in India in which a clan (advanced enough to acknowledge marriage and the patriarchal family and to cultivate in organised groups) *did* actually reclaim or cultivate land, in common, before allotting it in severalty among the members? I know of nothing resembling it. In the absence of any actual case of "common" holding on the part of such a tribe, the theoretical view of the meaning of the tribal custom of redistribution depends very much on some just appreciation of what ideas "of property" really are; and this we must at present defer.

It will be observed that even if this attempted reference of the widespread "severalty" village form to a Dravidian or Turanian origin is for any reason regarded as doubtful, there still remains the fact that no other suggestion has been made; and the objection that Sir H. Maine's theory fails to suit the real history of the large area of "severalty villages" remains as valid as ever, because it cannot be justified except (1) by showing some reasonable indications of a "common ownership"—the same as that in the north—and prevailing over the whole region of the severalty villages ; and (2) further, by showing that circumstances existed under the influence of which the loss of some features, and the acquisition of others, can be accounted for. The usual way in which the supposed change is explained is by a general assertion of "decay" of the joint form into the severalty. Thus Mr. J. D. Mayne, in his valuable book on "Hindu Law and Usage,"[1] repeating the usual suggestion that the severalty villages of the Dakhan were once communal "*like the villages of the Panjâb*," and that they have decayed into their present state, proposes as the cause, that "the wars and devastations of the Muhammedans, Maharattas, and Pindarries swept away the village institutions, as well as almost every form of ancient proprietary right." But as a matter of fact, such wars and devastations were just as common throughout Hindustân and the Panjâb where the joint village has been fully preserved ; and the view that "every form of ancient proprietary right" was swept away in the Dakhan cannot be sustained. I have already indicated the general character of the population of the peninsula (p. 47), and remarked on the absence of any considerable immigrations introducing extensive changes. When (from the fourteenth or fifteenth century) Muhammadan rule began, the tendency was rather to preserve

[1] 4th Ed., § 201, p. 219. This seems also to be the idea suggested in Sir G. Campbell's paper in the Cobden Club series.

village and other popular institutions.[1] The Mahrâthas also did not destroy the village forms; no indication of anything of the kind is presented either by the districts longest under Mahrâtha rule, or by those merely raided or subjected to an impost for a brief period. The object of that greedy and oppressive rule, no doubt, was to make heavy exactions which were levied without any regard to who found the money or how it was obtained. Instead of adhering to the old customary "Hindu" method of taking the share of the grain from each holder on each threshing floor (or taking an *estimated* amount from each as the later custom was) the Mahrâtha collector insisted on a total cash revenue from the village[2] for which he held the headman (or a manager) responsible. This very much upset individual rights; weak cultivators were driven out and better ones called in; the holdings were perhaps rearranged arbitrarily, and everybody had to contribute what he *could*, not merely what he *ought*. A series of holdings that had long been held in severalty would, under

[1] In Gujarât it was in the (Moslem) Nawâb's territory that the *narwâdâri* and other joint villages are *best* preserved. In Nimâr—the part of the Central Provinces which had known a continuous Moslem rule—the headman's *watan* land, and other such privileges likely to be the first to disappear, were observed to be *most* in evidence.

[2] This was usually the amount of the old Muhammadan valuation, made up, on one pretence or another, to a "full" or "perfect" (*kamâl*) assessment. It was of course not often realised in full; but there it was as the standard to be aimed at.

such treatment, lose all traces of union arising from a reminiscence of earlier days of tribal allotment. But such a system did not alter the whole village form, nor turn a "joint" village into a "severalty." On the contrary, it was very likely to *produce* (artificially) the joint form by causing the combination of the richer families (in some villages) as a joint body assuming ownership of the whole, or by establishing a revenue manager or tax farmer and his family as proprietor in others.[1] Privileges, like the free-landholding of the headman, tended to disappear; the hereditary rights attached to village offices were actually seized and held by Mahrâtha chiefs and *jâgîrdârs* for their own profit; but the *form of village* underwent no change.

The fact is that we should never have heard of this "decay" theory were it not for the circumstance that we had certain vestiges—easily misunderstood—of special rights in land in parts of the west and south. The holders of certain village lands in those places are (or once were) distinguished as *mirâsdâr*. It was imagined that these had been connected with a system of *collective ownership*, already believed to be universal; so that they must represent the once general form, and the ordinary severalty village was the result of their decay. Why a survival should have occurred

[1] This latter, however, the Mahrâthas rarely allowed; the moment a village manager, farmer, or official was known to be securing a position, they came down upon him at once.

only here and there, and completely failed or become obliterated elsewhere, was never explained, nor indeed could be.

As it would interrupt the exposition of the main objections to the theory to give *here* the explanation of the occasional appearances of villages held by joint bodies in the south, among the severalty villages, I have relegated a short summary of local facts to Appendix I.

I will conclude by resuming the position in a few words. The severalty village, uniformly found over a very large part of India, is not the result of any decay of a jointly owned village, or a village held and governed as the northern villages are. It is the natural—and *comparatively* little changed—result of an ancient settlement of the country under tribes of which the village groups formed small sections each under its leaders. When once the village site was determined on (perhaps existing sites [more or less cleared] were obtained by conquest) the chief, aided by the principal families, made an allotment of lands or holdings which were separately enjoyed, and which were not held "in common" in any real sense, though the villagers would obey their chief, unite for defence, and submit to any custom of periodic exchange of holdings in order to secure equal advantages to all. Then, in the long course of ages, the holdings became varied by the introduction of other families: the older tribal feeling of union died away, the exchange ceased to be practised, and the several holdings became not only separately held, but without any connecting link of tribal organisation; but the village form remained, the influential headman, and his *watan* land, in particular. Even if it is true that rudimentary groups of cultivation, undertaken by still more primitive groups of people on a matriarchal plan, did in some districts precede the more organic village of the kind described, that does not in any way justify the theory under discussion, which supposes a type of village held in common, and bearing the six features indicated—entirely unlike the suggested matriarchal groups within the *parhâ* of the primitive Kolarian.

(*b*) *The Theory with Reference to the Joint Villages of Northern India*

It is a curious feature of most writings on the subject of Indian villages, that they treat these interesting groups as if they were things in the air, and not existing institutions which can be enumerated and classified in one way or another. As regards Upper India more especially, where the "joint" type of village is prevalent, it can be definitely ascertained, in a large proportion of cases, who the village "communities" are, and how they came there (pp. 72-3). Sir H. Maine appears to have been satisfied with the general idea that the Indian population was "Aryan," and that all villages might be assumed to be Aryan, and therefore archaic and of one type. But we know that this is not the case; we know also that there are various forms of joint village in Northern India, all traceable to known races and (at least, approximately) to known periods of history. A certain number of villages, indeed, elude the attempt to determine their original plan of sharing, but the greater part can be accounted for. They are not anywhere distinctively Aryan (pp. 53, 72), but they were formed by tribes and families who had a sense of conquest and superiority, and a power of cohesion—which time has not yet quite destroyed—such as we may well suppose the Aryan tribes to have possessed.

We have noticed, as a fact, that the joint villages of the north, however classified for convenience of study, are essentially formed on one of two principles. Their "jointness" is due (1) either to the fact that the village was originally dominated or founded by some one (or more than one) superior or "overlord," and that the joint community is the expanded family following the custom of joint inheritance; or (2) it is due to the cohesiveness of groups who have been formed by clans or tribes settling and allotting the village land, on their own system, among themselves. Very often the apparent tribe is simply the expansion of one or more families which have gradually multiplied from a central or parent village, and formed numerous villages all in one contiguous group—often of great extent, and all of *common* descent—each local subdivision being naturally the closer kindred of the particular members who started it. Nearly allied to this class of (tribal) villages are those which are really voluntarily associated bodies who have allotted the land by consent, according to the number of persons in each household, or according to the number of cattle possessed, or the amount of money and labour contributed to sinking irrigation wells.

The theory we are examining correctly appreciates the union which these variously originating villages present, their ability to accept a joint responsibility for revenue and taxes, and their preservation of equality, by insisting on government by a committee of heads of families, not by an oligarchy of chiefs or by a single "headman"; but it has interpreted those features as meaning that the land was owned "in common" or "collectively" by the several families or houses in the village, and curiously insists that when the blood relationship of the village landholders is quite forgotten, they still hold together *by means of cultivation in common.* This "common" ownership is assumed to be an Aryan feature. As regards the latter point, it will probably be no longer defended by anyone. There is no evidence that the early Aryan tribes had any idea of the common ownership of land except that they possessed (as seems probable) the custom of the joint family and the joint inheritance of the members in succession to the head. The connection of the idea of family joint ownership with common ownership in general will be considered later on. And whether or not the Aryans had any general institution of "common" property, the fact remains that the villages now in the joint form have little if any connection with the early Aryans at all (p. 57).

Still, whatever the nationality, the villages certainly exhibit features of union; and with reference to *point* 2. (p. 99) it is proper at once to inquire how far the phenomena of this union warrant any assertion of "collective ownership" as its original form or source.

It does not seem to me that the theory has ever been supported by any explicit statement as to what is meant by "holding in common"; and that sometimes *joint*-holding, which appears to be quite distinct, is confused with it.

I can only think of a really "common" holding, when each person concerned has no idea at all of any ownership—divided or undivided—residing in himself, but only in the group; when no one has any share that he calls his own, but all co-operate in tilling the fields, to supply the whole group, or to furnish a common granary or a common fund, on which each family draws, merely according to its wants, which may be greater or less according to numbers. It is perhaps hardly necessary to observe that no vestige of such a mode of enjoyment of land can be observed or traced in any North Indian village; further, that no organised village exists, or ever has existed—as far as any evidence goes—in which a definite lot or share in the village lands for each member of the community has not always been known.[1] In some cases where the co-owners are the heirs of one owner or founder, the shares have not been divided out on the ground, and the holding continues joint (p. 79). I am convinced that it is partly the mistaking of "joint" holding of co-sharers for a "communal" idea of property, and partly the mistranslation of one of the office-terms,[2] that has led to the idea of any of these villages being held "in common." It is worth while to explain this mistake. In the 5th Section (p. 62) we saw that a large class of villages exists in which one man (or perhaps two or three brothers) had obtained the proprietorship over the village. Villages of this class were called

[1] I need hardly allude to the mention of "some parts" of (Upper) India (but neither named nor localised), in one of the Fragments of Nearchos, of which he reports that the people cultivated by means of their families in common (*κατὰ συγγέναιαν κοινῇ*), and after distributing the grain necessary to satisfy the wants of the several households, destroyed the rest! Even this does not describe common ownership, but joint family life. See Lassen *Indische Altertumskunde*, ii., p. 727, (2nd Edit.), and F. de Coulanges "Origin of Property," Mrs. Ashley's Translation, p. 113 (Swan Sonnenschein & Co., 1891).

[2] This is evident in Mr. J. D. Mayne's "Hindu Law and Usage," p. 200, when he alludes to the "communal *zamîndâri*."

zamîndâri, which means "landlord" (village). But such owners invariably followed the law or custom of joint inheritance, so that in the process of time it was a matter of course that (not any single heir but) a growing body of co-sharing heirs should take the place of the founder. If then these (constituting the "community") had not happened to divide the inheritance, they formed a joint landlord body; but the tenure was exactly the same as in the first stage, except for the number; and the office term for it was *zamîndâri mushtarka*, or the landlord village where the superior interest is held by an undivided co-parcenary body. The words have nothing whatever to do with "communal" ownership. When such joint heirs partitioned their estate, the shares were necessarily according to the ancestral scale which follows from the place in the table of descent (see Diagram, p. 77). Exactly the same development occurred in all that class of villages—some earlier, some later, in point of time—in which there is a single dominant family from which the existing proprietary body originated. The real truth seems to be that the idea of "communal" holding—whatever may be meant by it—has been practically derived from this one class of "joint" village (which has been alluded to as "manorial"), ignoring the tribal and associate forms altogether. The mere consideration of these facts seems enough to show that there is nothing really in the nature of a holding "in common" or "collectively."

But if such common holding cannot be asserted even in the case of a joint family however expanded, what shall we say of that other large group of "joint" villages (still referring only to the cases of *known* origin) in which there is no appearance of the manorial growth, but the joint group is of the one or other of the various origins stated at pp. 85-95, and where (it will be recollected) shares or lots have been arranged, declared, and possessed, from the beginning of the village, and where the methods of allotment are different from those in the "manorial" family village, and are sometimes curious and specific, sometimes mere holdings adapted to the wants of each sharer. Reference of these diverse forms to a single original type is simply out of the question; it is inconsistent with facts. In some of these forms, it is clear, no trace of common ownership can be discovered, and we must resort to the most unwarrantable assumptions to make out that such a thing ever existed. It is true that in this division we have included the important class (*e.g.*, the tribal villages on the north-west frontier and elsewhere, p. 87) in which there has been a tribal allotment of lands among the members of a settling and immigrant clan. And here the principle is just the same as that which I have argued to be the basis of the original severalty village among the Dravidian population of peninsular India. Only that in these northern parts circumstances and the character of the people have preserved a greater unity of race and the ability to unite in sustaining a common responsibility. Indeed this class of village only needs to be examined in detail, and it will at once be apparent that there is nothing in the nature of cultivation in common, although a part of the estate, being waste and kept for grazing, may be held as the common property because (until it is wanted for cultivation) its utility would be diminished by partition. Nor can we assume, in the absence of any evidence, that any holding "in common" preceded such allotment for cultivation. And if here also, a custom of re-distribution or periodical exchange of holdings is observed, or is believed to have existed at some former time, the value of this as an indication of "common ownership" has already been discussed (p. 104). The custom (*a*) of joint inheritance and (*b*) of restricting the ownership of land to the agnatic group, or at least within the tribe, are not indications of "common ownership."

These remarks incidentally dispose of the view (point 4, p. 100) that the existence of "shares" or "lots" for cultivation is due to some kind of later modification—some stage supervening on a primitive holding in common. Shares were always known; the very principle of the joint family (where that was the basis) implies it. Shares (of another kind) were also the original and necessary feature of that class of village which was last alluded to.

But there is one later development of the theory regarding shares (for which Sir H. S. Maine is in no way responsible) which is altogether illusory. It is that the (imagined) common holding has been changed by a serial "evolution"—first, a "common" holding, then "regular" (*i.e.*, ancestral) shares, and then "customary" shares, custom having modified the original fractional (ancestral) shares scheme. This, in most cases, is distinctly and historically inconsistent with fact. The (real) *bhaiâchârâ* or "customary" sharing (p. 88) as well as the modes of allotment *other* than the "ancestral" share-system, are independent schemes evidently due to a special feeling of equality and membership right among the clan or other group. Nothing can be said in favour of the view that they are decayed forms of the "ancestral" share.[1]

[1] Indeed, Mr. J. D. Mayne would never have broached the idea but for the unfortunate misuse of the term *bhaiâchârâ*, in the official returns, to *include* (among others) villages where the holdings are *now* merely *de facto*, but are known or believed to have become so by the loss (under adverse circumstances) of the correct ancestral shares. Even here, though we have a case of decay, it does not mark an "evolution" of any kind: it is merely the effect of time and accident in altering the extent of some of the shares in particular cases. Such cases are undoubtedly common. Indeed, it is rather the exception to find the "ancestral" shares preserved in absolute correctness. But this very natural "wear and tear" does not alter the principle; and it is a great mistake to mix up these cases with another class where the "customary" share is on a perfectly definite principle of its own, and indicates a different mode of growth.

But I must hasten to notice the further contention (point 2, p. 99), which would compel us to infer that "common holding" must once have existed, even where allotment has long taken place, because the separate holdings are, it is supposed, still cultivated in common or in a certain way, under control of the elders. It must be observed, shortly, that the existence of any such control is a pure imagination. In the (rare) cases where there has been no permanent allotment, and the cultivation is arranged for year by year, there will, of course, be a preliminary agreement as to what fields each is to work, and how the payment of burdens is to be made: that can hardly be what is meant. But in all cases where partition has taken place, or where separate lots have always been held, everyone cultivates exactly as he pleases, subject only to a settlement of his proportionate payment of the revenue, etc., if that is not already fixed. As to "minute" or "multifarious" rules, intended "to reconcile the holding of separate fields with the idea of common cultivation," I should be completely at a loss to imagine how the idea of such a thing originated, except that Sir H. S. Maine gives us a clue by showing that he derived it from the cases he had heard of, of irrigated villages where the whole of the holdings, sometimes comprising a number of scattered plots, had to be watered from a single source. Sometimes this is a canal cut, or locally a stream, or a torrent only occasionally flowing for limited periods. Sometimes a number of plots are watered from one well. In such cases rules, or schemes of days and hours, and turns at the well, or the order of damming up the stream or watercourse, are arranged (both for owners and tenants), and they may appear complicated. These, no doubt, are not matters of mere give-and-take—of independent contract,[1] because they all proceed on a well-known existing scheme of shares and separate rights; and such arrangements are obviously necessary when the source is one and the claimants many.[2] That the scheme of distribution is often arranged without difficulty[3] indicates a good deal of tribal or of family union, or village solidarity, as the case may be; but how it indicates an idea of "common cultivation" I fail to perceive. In other respects, cultivation of separate holdings is entirely free; old-established agricultural rules and modes are usually followed,

1 "V. C.," p. 109. The author, it will be remembered, regarded *shares* as a sort of later invention, so that he could not account for the ready settlement of all questions as to use of irrigation water. Certainly it was not arranged as a mere business contract, *because* it all depends on the existing and well-known shares; but ignoring this fact, the author thought it must depend on some idea of "*common* cultivation."

2 In some of the north-west frontier districts it sometimes happens that the land is of no value without water; in that case the rights of the co-sharer are expressed in terms of water-shares, the land is not regarded at all. Anyone can take a plot of land, but it is of no use unless he has a water-share.

3 But not always; bitter enmities and fierce quarrels sometimes arise out of the matter.

but no one ever heard of a separate landholder being controlled or directed in his cultivation by the *panchâyat* or by anyone else.

Under this head I ought, perhaps, to mention that in most villages where the sharers are of the same clan or are kinsmen, a custom of *pre-emption* prevails. This has nothing to do with cultivating in common, but is a device to prevent strangers getting into the village as purchasers of land, wherever there is a blood-relation or a co-sharing connection willing to take the land offered for sale at a fair value. It is merely the expression of that desire to preserve the union of a family, or of clansmen, which is naturally expected in any village which has a really joint character.

It will perhaps be asked: If there is no common cultivation, what is it that holds the village together? I reply that it is the fact of common tribe and often of common family, with the customs that the remembrance of the fact preserves; reinforced, too, by recollection of past days when union preserved the villages, alike in their internecine feuds and against the armies that traversed the northern plains, and against the revenue-farmers. Indeed, I think Sir H. S. Maine is inclined very much to underrate the reality of the common descent of village bodies, or at least a very practical belief in it, in a large class of cases.[1] No doubt artificial additions to the families

[1] See point 5, at p. 101, and quotations there given.

may be made by adoption, or in some cases by giving the family Brahman a share, or by calling in relations on the female side to help, and giving them shares; and these occurrences may sometimes lead to a denial of this or that particular relationship as shown in the genealogical tree; but that does not make the family groups *generally* artificial, and in many cases the "genealogical tree" is one of the most instructive records in the volume of Settlement papers, and explains the shares of the village body most completely. In these cases actual family feeling does come in a good deal; and in others there is a wider sense of clan union, which is something of the same kind. It is really only in a limited class of cases that we can say "consanguinity" has nothing to do with it.[1]

And this naturally leads to the last point in the theory (No. 6, p. 101)—the structure of the community itself. It is, of course, true that in one sense we may speak of the "community" as including everyone permanently resident in, or serving the village; and thus there are varieties of caste and rank—artisans, village officers, tenants, and proprietors. If wronged, the tenants and village helpers

[1] See "Ind. Vill. Comm.," p. 274, for an example where separate families are aggregated, but the wider *tribal* feeling still unites them; or again, in the North Panjâb, where wholly separate groups combined, each having a separate *tarf* or quarter in the village (*id.* p. 339). Here the bond is voluntary union for defence.

would find their cause locally espoused, and protection and countenance readily afforded. But when it comes to including all classes in the "brotherhood,' that is quite contrary to the facts. Indeed, the idea of a proud Râjput kindred or group of, say 80 or 100 co-sharing members, with 15 or 20 elders or heads of houses, regarding their cultivating tenants and the village watchmen, not to mention the washerman and the sweeper, as constituting part of the "brotherhood," is something quite grotesque. This "brotherhood" does not constitute any graded "hierarchy" in any case whatever, nor has it any social strata in parallel layers, representing the successive "amalgamation" of groups at remote periods. The "brotherhood" consists of just as many families as have actual shares in the land—as are existing co-proprietors, and no more (see pp. 60 *note*, 75).

The mistake, however, was a not unnatural one, and may have arisen partly from a reminiscence of a feature in these villages which is of real interest. I have mentioned the possibility of persons outside the agnatic group being admitted to a share. Sometimes, too, at a not very remote period, under pressure of some extravagant demand for revenue from a local governor, a number of persons will have been invited on to the land to help cultivation, with the promise of never being asked to pay more than the proprietors themselves paid; but, even so, I doubt whether these privileged helpers would be considered as actually a part of the "brotherhood." It is possible also that after a long course of harsh exaction—such as the Sikh rule produced in the Panjâb—difference of origin may have been forgotten. In those times, it is well-known, the officials made no distinction between proprietor and tenant—they took from every one on the land, the utmost farthing that could be got. Separate grades of right might then become confused; and ultimately, when the village was settled under happier auspices, the "brotherhood," or the group of co-sharers actually in possession of holdings, might be allowed to include some families of different descent. But that is not always, or even frequently, the case. So generally is the distinction between proprietary and non-proprietary holders observed, that very often cases have occurred where a real proprietor has left the village in debt—which debt his fellows have had to make good—and he has sought re-entry after many years. In that case, unless he pays up the money, he will very likely be re-admitted only to the holding of his own former fields, but without a voice in the management or any share in profits—he remains outside the "brotherhood."

I must not omit to add a word about the *tenants* in such villages, for it is the existence of degrees of right and privilege of this class that has led, principally, to the idea of parallel layers or strata in the social constitution of communities. But let it be said at once that tenants, even those paying no rent (only the revenue share), are only tenants—not part of the "brotherhood." It may be, and often is, the case—for instance, in the Râjput communities of the N.W. Provinces—that the tenants are descendants of older cultivating settlers who once had independent rights, over whom the landlord family established its superiority. In other cases the "tenants" are a body of lower caste (or poorer high caste) cultivators and dependents, established by the founder or proprietary-family in the virgin waste, where there was no already existing body of cultivators. And then there may not only be these two groups of interest, but a third or more. For suppose a family settled in a village as "overlords" over an earlier group, and soon fully recognised as landlords. After a longer or shorter term of prosperity, this body has become overborne by some new conquest or usurpation; then the new-comers will crystallise into the actual "proprietary brotherhood," and the others will sink down into the tenant rank, only not so completely as those first-mentioned, and will perhaps retain rights of occupancy or other privilege.[1] But only the "actual proprietors" of the time constitute the "brotherhood." In all these matters the theory misrepresents the actual joint village almost as seriously as it fails to

[1] It was the recurrence of this sort of growth and overgrowth of rights—the super-imposition of one interest over another—that led to the complications of tenant-right and the variety of claims that had to be settled by the Legislature.

correspond with the facts regarding the severalty type. I fear there is no disguising the truth that the theory is based on a radically defective view of the real principles which underlie the formation of either kind of village.

VII

IDEAS OF "PROPERTY" OR "OWNERSHIP"

THERE are a few general observations to be made regarding the development of ideas of property in land; and how far "common" or "collective" ownership can be regarded as a natural thing; and what is the effect of the "joint family" custom among agricultural tribes. There are also some reflections which occur as to the practical uses of the "village" form of landholding and its social and economic aspects.

From one point of view the idea of property "in common" is not a primitive or simple one. It may be taken to imply a prior recognition of what "property" or "ownership" *is;* and that, again, involves such an analysis as the Roman lawyers made when they considered the intentions and powers existing in relation to land or other objects, which distinguished an "owner" from a person who might have certain rights, and yet not be the owner. The right to use, the right to destroy, the right to alienate, the right to enjoy the produce, the right to defend the property against aggression, these combined and permanent rights may originate in various ways.

Until some such conception is realised (and that is not likely in a very primitive stage), and there is a law and a system of public justice to recognise and enforce it, "ownership," it may be urged, can hardly be said to exist at all. It is when "ownership" is regularly understood, that there arises the further conception that the exercise of such a right may reside in one person or in a body of co-sharers—whether divided in fact or not—or it may reside in a "common" holding, in a body with no shares, but all receiving from the common fund such amount as is needed for their support, without a thought that this man (from his place in the family or otherwise) has a right to one-third or one-twentieth, or any other certain proportion.

On the other hand, it may be urged that, as a matter of fact, long before any such legal conception is elaborated, the earliest of mankind easily acquire an undefined but operative sense of ownership, which they manifest by having a natural consciousness of a sufficient justification, when they expel or put to death enemies who should attempt to graze cattle, to dig wells, to cut trees, or to cultivate the soil, within the understood limits of their settlement. This undefined idea of ownership seems to arise, naturally, from some sense of labour undergone, or skill or valour exercised, in the acquisition. At a time when almost boundless forest covers the land, no one is likely to regard a tree as more the subject of ownership than the air or the water of a great river. But let one man fell a tree, and prepare from the trunk a canoe, a rudely ornamented cup or platter, or a club, and he naturally conceives himself entitled to the product of his workmanship in a way that no one else is. And it is the same with a plot of land. A man and his family laboriously clear it, dig up the stumps, level it, and make it into a maize field; they are felt to have (in some sense) a special right to it, though no one could yet define the elements of the conception of such ownership. And it depends on how the labour is expended, whether it is by an individual or a group, that the right is felt to reside in the individual or the group. It is well-known that in the only place where the "Laws of Manu" allude to a right in land, the title is an individual one, and is attributed to the natural source—still so universally acknowledged throughout India—that a man was the first to remove the stumps and prepare the land for the plough. At the same time we see, from very early times, how the grain produce of every allotment is not all taken by the owner of the land, but part of it is by custom assigned to this or that recipient. It is not, observe, that the land allotment itself is not completely separated; but when the crop is reaped, the owner (as we may call him) at once recognised that out of his grain heap at the threshing floor, not only the great chief or Râjâ, and his own immediate headman, but a variety of other villagers, have customary rights to certain shares—if it is only sometimes a few double handfuls or other small measure. All this seems to spring from the sense of co-operation (however indirect) in the work of settlement that made the holding possible.[1] It seems to me quite clear that a sense of individual "property" in land may arise coincidently with a sense of a certain right in others to have a share of the produce (on the ground of co-operation), and that the two are not felt to conflict. So far, the natural sentiment is one rather of individual right, tempered by the obligation to give part of the produce to helpers and rulers, or for the needs of pious charity or worship.

But settlements of agriculturists, in early times especially, do not usually begin with one man or one family clearing a patch in an unoccupied country. A clan group, or perhaps a still larger body, has marched to the place and has taken possession, either because the land was uncleared or unoccupied, or because an enemy has been expelled or enslaved. Then the feeling is that every tribesman who has taken part in the adventure must have his equal share. And it is an observed fact (which will demand separate notice) that often when a "close kindred" or existing family gets a lot, there is a further internal sense of owner-

[1] This subject has been very well dealt with in Mr. W. C. Benett's "Settlement Report of Gonda" (Oudh), p. 44, sec. 74. See my "Ind. Vill. Comm.," p. 16. It will be observed that Mr. Benett is speaking of the customary grain shares in a village which is purely and completely in severalty.

ship by the whole family, which is in abeyance as long as the head lives, but which takes effect (again in *equal* division) as soon as the head dies. "Shares" in a village area, as I have already said, are no after-thought; they invariably arise coevally with the appropriation of the site. In one class of cases they arise out of the equal allotment of the territory among the tribesmen, the clan, and the smaller group. No such thing as common holding can be traced for a time previous to such allotment; it is made as soon as possible, or goes on continuously as the numbers grow. In another class of cases shares arise from the fact that a particular person or family of distinction has dominated the village, and the "family" together is regarded as a unit which is known to consist of sons, grandsons, and great-grandsons,[1] each of whose proportional right depends on his birth and place in the table of descent. It is really this latter class alone that furnished our theorists with their idea of the Indian village in general.

It becomes necessary, then, to inquire a little into this matter of the "joint family," and how the conception arises that the undefined sort of "ownership," of which I have spoken, attaches (at least

[1] "Ind. Vill. Comm.," p. 233 ff. And this class of cases appears always in connection with the rise and progress of monarchical ideas, and of the baronies and feudal jurisdictions which accompany it. Individual grantees, or mere usurpers, gain in the *village* a petty "overlordship," as greater chiefs gain it over a wider territory.

in some tribes and regions) to the family as a whole.

The custom that a body of agnates are co-heirs, that the father is head while he lives, but that his sons have inchoate rights with him from the moment of their birth, is one that is not distinctively Aryan. It is prominent in all the later agricultural tribes of the north—Jat, Gujar, Râjput, etc. It is especially held to where the family has pretensions to rank and dignity; but even should it be modified in some respects in the more "democratic" clans or castes, still it affects the inheritance in the separated lots just as much as it may effect the constitution of a property embracing the whole village. The same custom is observed by the Muhammadan tribes—many of whom it is true are converts; but it is also followed by Pathâns and others, who were always Moslem. The fact is that the strict Muhammadan law of inheritance, with its complicated exclusions of one branch in the presence of another, and so forth, must have arisen among a people whose property was chiefly in camels and merchandise, and perhaps houses; it is entirely unsuited to dealing with ancestral land. So much is certain that the joint family custom can exist in various forms, and need not exist at all.

Possibly the Roman idea of the father as absolute owner, and of his children as having no rights at all, until they are emancipated or pass out of his hands by marriage, is a later and quite special development. It never appeared, as far as we know, in India.

As known to our Hindu law books, and to the decisions of the Privy Council, the joint family is a much more elaborated and more religious institution than as it exists among the agricultural communities. In the same way the law of adoption, as known to the Hindu commentators, is rather widely different to the custom prevailing among agrarian tribes. The whole custom is directed to preserving land in the male agnate line; or, at least (if that fails), in the wider kindred. Hence alienation is restricted; and so is adoption, which practically might act as a kind of alienation out of the line of customary heirs.

One of the interesting questions concerning the joint family is whether the earlier Dravidian tribes in India possessed it? It does not seem necessarily to belong to a state of life in which the *patriarchal* régime is established, though the rule as found in Hindu law, or in any of the Northern agricultural tribes, is certainly on a *patriarchal* basis. There is reason to believe that the Kolarian tribes were once *matriarchal*, and yet the little groups of descendants from a common mother might form a house communion, which is a kind of enlarged joint family. That any of the real Turanians or Dravidians of Central and Southern India were at one time matriarchal, does not seem to me at all ascertained. And the later, organised, tribes to whom I have attributed the origin of the "severalty" village, were certainly not so. If, as seems probable, they came from countries not far removed from the original home of the Aryan tribes, and some of them were more or less contemporaneous with the Yâdava and other Aryans in their invasion of India, it certainly seems likely that they had a *patriarchal* organisation, as the Aryans (of the Veda) certainly had. If the later dominant Turanian tribes had exhibited a *matriarchal* plan of relationship, it seems unlikely that it would escape all mention in early literature. More, of course, cannot be said.[1] Whatever definitely Dravidian custom we have traces of is on a patriarchal basis. Among the Kândhs, for example, the father holds the family lot in complete control during his life; and his sons, even when adult, live and work with him, forming a kind of house communion; only after his death they will share the property equally. It is expressly stated that "the sons have no property during their

[1] I am aware that a caste in Mâlabâr—the ruling (or military) race called Nâyar, of unknown origin, but possibly later Dravidian—have the custom of inheritance in the female line; the heirs are the sister's sons, and the joint family may consist of any number of descendants from a common mother. But this was a very special and alien dominant caste; its joint relationship has always been connected with maintenance of dignity; the rules of the whole institution are essentially unlike those of the Hindu law. It may well be doubted whether the custom is really ancient and not taken on in connection with the peculiar relations of the tribe to the Nambûri Brahmans. Curiously enough, we know it to have been (artificially) adopted by the local "Moplah" of Arabian origin.

father's lifetime."[1] Nor is any restriction mentioned as to the father's alienating land. The Chota-Nagpore village organisation too (p. 66) is certainly patriarchal.

Among the Jat, Râjput, and other tribes settled in the Panjâb, the custom is also certainly patriarchal; but here the father cannot alienate ancestral land (except under pressure of necessity) without the consent of the family; and in general his power of defeating the expectation of collaterals (where he has no son) by making an adoption, is variously restricted. Evidently the custom of a joint family is closely connected with the future joint inheritance. If a man acquires a village by grant or purchase, and proceeds, with the aid of his sons and servants, to improve the waste, to acquire first this and then that holding, and so become owner of the whole, it may be thought that he is naturally entitled to dispose of the whole as "acquired" by himself alone; but the sons, having helped in the establishment of the property, will probably regard themselves as having a title to share in it, by virtue of participation in the work of "founding"; and so, in the first degree, there is not much risk of the estate being lost before it comes to be inherited by anyone. And when once the land has descended to heirs, the next and following series will regard it as "ancestral." It is note-

[1] "Ind. Vill. Comm.," pp. 172, 173; and see the Report quoted in Hunter's "Orissa" II., p. 72.

worthy that the superior (dominating) families and the conquering tribes always speak of their ownership right (whether in the family or in the clan at large) as "the inheritance" (*wirâsat*, *mirâsi*, etc.). In these cases the feeling that actuates a whole clan seems, in part, at least, to be the same as that which appears in the microcosm of a single close-kindred. They are (ideally) joint-heirs of the common ancestor, and as all represent him, all take their share. And this is combined with the feeling that all have expended labour, skill, or money, and have perhaps undergone personal risk, and so are still further entitled, on this ground, to an equal share. Whether this is an equal share *per capita* at the moment of dividing the acquisition, or whether it is the share that follows from the grade in the table of descent, depends on the nature and origin of the family, or the clan group, whether they have a monarchical, "feudal," system or not.

We cannot tell whence the joint family and joint inheritance rules long observed in India were originally derived. We know of no time when the custom can be affirmed to have been non-existent among the tribes who formed the villages of Northern India.

As regards the general progress of ideas of ownership in India, we may resume the whole subject by saying that it is quite possible—and indeed almost certain—that we have first to allow for a nomadic stage, which gradually passes into an elementary form of village settlements, or rather of little groups of hamlets, each having a patch of cultivation only for its own common purposes; and that here it is likely that a (barbarous) matriarchal rule will subsist. The people gather at a festival, and the men of one village form temporary connections with the women of another (as Mr. Hewitt has described). The children born know only their mothers, and become the "children of the village," in which the males (who are not their fathers) are the managers. No hereditary or permanent chief can exist; but some one of the more capable persons is chosen as the managing head. In such a stage, "property" can hardly exist at all; and there is little objection to say that cultivation is practised for the common support of the local group. But the time comes when more advanced tribes, having the idea of marriage, and consequently of "the family," and of patriarchal society (with its elders and chiefs), obtain the upper hand; and then it is that we see more a complete village, divided into allotments, but still subject to customs of tribal union and redistribution of holdings — to secure equality—becoming organised. This village it is that originates the plan of the allotted or "severalty" village, which is the commonest form. In still later times another series of tribes, or families with the joint inheritance custom, dominate Upper India; and it is their family law, or their idea of allotting land to each member of the tribe or clan, that produces the form of "joint" village known in the north.

The early condition of landed property in village groups is not then one of "communal ownership," but is one dependent on the tribal organisation of society which provides an equal subsistence lot for every member of the tribe. And if this is followed by further developments of joint family inheritance and the domination of particular aristocratic or influential families, we have co-sharing brotherhoods claiming landlord rights. Moreover, in all cases the circumstances of life demand a close union for defence, so that, whether by tribal aggregation or family union, or by voluntary association, the joint or cohesive village as we see it in the North of India is preserved.

VIII

SOME PRACTICAL ASPECTS OF VILLAGE INSTITUTIONS

IT remains only to make a few remarks as to the social and political advantages (or disadvantages) arising from the village organisation of agrarian society, whether that organisation is in the form of the severalty village under a headman, or a body which, organised under joint family custom, or under some other form of tribal or family allotment, is in some sense "joint" and dealt with as a "proprietary unit" by the Administration.

In early days, whenever a district came under the N.W. Provinces authorities, the system required the village to be dealt with as a whole, as an unit, whether it was so naturally or not; and the method of the (so-called) *raiyatwâri* provinces, where each holding was dealt with separately, was regarded by officials trained in the north-western school with something like horror.[1] But all that has long passed away.

[1] Even Sir H. Maine, who was too philosophically minded to suppose that it was really wrong, says—contrary to all historical fact—that it was not the ancient system of the country ("V. C.,"

With the later well-organised establishments, it is just as easy to deal with thousands of separate holdings, grouped in villages, as it is to deal with a number of whole villages. And we have two Land-Revenue systems—one treating the village as a whole (but carefully recording all shares and separate rights), the other frankly adapted to the severalty village of the peninsula, and assessing each holding in complete independence.

The village organisation of society—whether the village itself is of one type or the other—offers many facilities for rural administration, for repression of crime, and gradually for bringing about attention to simple systems of sanitation. The village system also enables the agrarian districts to dispense with a poor law. Each village will secure its infirm and pauper inhabitants at least from starvation, without the intervention of any poor-rate machinery.

Moreover, the district officers are much more readily brought into friendly contact with the people, from village to village; each brings forward a new group of headmen and local elders, from whom the state of the country, the prevalence of sickness or cattle disease, or suffering from drought, or local famine, can be at once known. A vast number of

p. 106). What *was*, we may ask, the ancient system, if it was not the taking of a share of the grain from every separate holding in each village, under the superintendence of the headman and the king's agent or accountant—the village itself being usually in the *raiyatwâri* form? See the note to p. 70.

separate points of communication exist, and the whole area of a district is divided up into small sections, which can be examined one by one, just as an engraver divides a picture he has to copy into little squares, so as to concentrate attention, and direct it successively to every section in detail. In parts of Bengal, for example, the district officer is almost dependent on the police officers scattered about at local stations for information regarding the country affairs. There are no other points of communication: the village organisation has almost completely decayed under the influence of the greater landlords. This, however, does not apply so much to those parts where the landowners are really peasant proprietors, and no *large* estates exist.

The village system produces all the advantages, but also the disadvantages, of "peasant proprietorship" in their full extent. For whether it is a separate (individual) holding, or a whole village regarded as the estate of a joint group, the land may be subdivided again and again, till the ultimate holding is so small that it barely affords the means of subsistence. In much-divided joint villages, especially where the plan of division is at all complicated, the whole of the co-sharers are really in the hands of the village accountant (*patwâri*), who alone knows all the details of the little scattered plots, and the charge upon each. The joint village is also peculiarly liable to develop cliques and parties, and even to split into fierce factions; and the co-sharer in one *patti*, or section, hates the members of another section cordially.[1] The success of the northern village largely depends on the energy and character of the tribe or family group holding it. There is a vast difference—I must say superiority—for example, when one compares the villagers of the West Panjâb with those of Ambâla, or—farther east—of Aligarh (for example), or of Bihâr: not that each race may not have some conspicuous good qualities of its own.

When the village or the holding becomes much subdivided, the holders are sure to get into debt. If the clan, caste, or tribe is of a good fibre, it does not allow such excessive subdivision: the energetic members, who see that all cannot thrive on the paternal inheritance, take service in the army, the police, or the numerous branches of minor public service; but even so, the supply of occupation is limited, because all crafts and industries are so tied to particular castes and hereditary groups and guilds that any general turning of surplus hands to industrial occupations is hardly possible.[2]

But when a landholder gets into debt he generally ends by mortgaging his land, and finally selling it.

1 I have noticed this more particularly in the Panjâb, north of the Gujrânwâla district.

2 Something can, of course, be done in this direction, especially in helping the village women to take up embroidery and other such work as they are naturally skilled in, to help out the family maintenance.

This does not always, or even frequently, involve his removal. The purchaser, unless he is a richer co-sharer (under the operation of the custom of *pre-emption* which prevails in many villages) will frequently be the village money-lender, or some non-resident banker desirous of accumulating land as an investment. The old owner or co-sharer resides still on the land, only he is now the tenant of the purchaser. This plan is not likely to answer very long if the holding is such that it does not afford more profit than suffices to support the tenant's family. The tendency must be either for a whole village to fall piecemeal into the hands of some (non-agricultural) owner, or else it will become held by absentee money-lenders and traders of various origin, and having no connection one with the other.

It may seem strange that in the progress of ideas regarding the State's dealing with the land in India, it never occurred to anyone to utilise, rather than abandon, the State ownership of the land. It is well known that when land administration first came under the direct control of British officers in Bengal in the eighteenth century, it was a firmly-established doctrine that the State was the owner of all land. Mr. James Grant, in Bengal, even argued that this was legal and constitutional; and it is not certain whether Lord Cornwallis took this view or not. It is not necessary here to discuss the question as it may be argued from the texts of the Hindu or

Muhammadan law. It is quite enough to remember that long before the eighteenth century, *de facto* the right had been fully established, and is asserted to this day by all the native states.[1] Lord Cornwallis simply desired to abandon it, substituting the *Zamindâr* landlords, whom he found in managing possession of large estates in Central Bengal. These he hoped to see acting the part of benevolent owners, at once securing the State revenues and blessing their tenants by their liberality and kind dealing. When, in the N.W. Provinces (in the absence of such landlords), attention was turned to establishing the independent rights of the villages, it was still the policy to give up the State right. The "joint body," dealt with as the ideal landlord of the village, is not declared by the Regulation (of 1822), in so many words, to be "actual proprietor"; but this right is implied, and the whole body, as well as the several co-sharers, are treated in all respects as owners. Not only so, but when in Bombay and Madras the individual holding was separately dealt with (without the intervention of any middleman proprietor or joint responsibility), and when the supreme ownership of the State was maintained, or at least not formally abrogated,[2] still

[1] See "Ind. Vill. Comm.," p. 207 ff. It is quite possible, no doubt, to find in Sanskrit books passages which contain vague assertions of the king's power, and of his being owner of everything; but it would be beyond the scope of this little book to enter on the discussion of such a matter.

[2] It is expressly maintained under the terms of the Bombay

no restriction was placed on the power of alienating the permanent hereditary occupancy, which for all practical purposes was as good as ownership. It might have occurred to someone in authority to think that the State ownership should be formally retained for beneficial purposes, to prevent the ignorant agricultural classes from losing their lands. The State would, in fact, have retained the *nuda proprietas*—the bare ownership of the soil—while giving all the practical benefits to the village co-sharer or the ryot cultivator; and the effect would have been that the holder could not sell the land which was not his; and moreover, by express enactment it might have been provided that he should not sell (or charge beyond his own lifetime) the occupancy or cultivating right in the holding.

As it is, the "ryot," no less than the co-sharing proprietor of the north, is free to lose his right by mortgaging and ultimately selling it. Thus many agriculturists have got into debt, and their lands became hopelessly encumbered, under either system. I am not saying that this complete *laissez faire* to

Revenue Code. In Madras, where no such code has been enacted, it is more or less tacitly or inferentially maintained, because it is so essentially a part of the system (formerly of great practical importance) that any "occupant" may relinquish his land by notice at a suitable season, and thus become free of the responsibility to pay the land-revenue. While this is maintained, it would be inconsistent to call the "occupant" or "ryot" the full *owner* of his holding.

the ordinary action of economic forces was or was not right; but no one seriously considered any other view. The "Ryots Relief Acts"[1] and similar provisions have rarely had any great success. To some extent this is due to the fact that they require very exceptional qualities in the officers who work them—sympathy, resource, great knowledge of local conditions and the like. But the provisions at best can only touch a part of the evil. When the debt burdening the share, or holding, is examined, it is usually found to consist of a vast mass of interest piled up; and the whole matter is complicated by the fact that the debtor's payments on account have been mostly in kind, that even if these have been fully credited in respect of quantity—which is by no means always the case—the money-lender has put his own market value on the credit items. The unfortunate debtor disputes both the smallness of the quantity and the meagreness of the value allowed him; but, alas! he has no evidence;—no receipts, no regular accounts of his own; and when the arbitrating judges come to settle the account, though they can reduce the interest easily enough, they can only deal with the items of the principal account, almost by guess. And even if the debt is reduced to a reasonable, and *per se* tolerably accurate, figure, it may well be that the

[1] They have been applied both in parts of the N.W. Provinces and in the Dakhan for the relief of encumbered village owners, and for ryots whose holdings have become burdened with debt.

holding is not capable of yielding enough to support the family, and also to give a surplus for the instalment of the debt besides the revenue and rates. In that case the fixing of the debt, and even the advance of the whole from the public treasury—to be repaid by fixed instalments constituting a first charge on the land, and extending over a number of years, at moderate (simple) interest—does not really relieve the holding, unless the mouths to be fed from it can be largely reduced; and this is rarely practicable. We have recently heard of proposals to restrict the alienation of land in India. The difficulty is how—after the free property system has gone on so long—to introduce any change. I am only here speaking of villages, and therefore do not allude to the cases of landlords in Madras, Oudh, etc., where primogeniture prevails, and the owner may have no power to alienate or charge the estate beyond his own lifetime. But in the peasant class, any attempt to deal with the subject by a *general* law would, I fear, result in a great difficulty. If any change is made, it must be very cautiously in separate provinces, and even separate districts, and experimentally—first where the conditions are such that it could be tried with the least appearance of a violent *bouleversement.* Especially where many holdings have already passed into the hands of money-lenders and others, an inquiry, unless very cautiously conducted, might have the effect of stirring up alarm and spreading excitement over the towns, in which the monied and trading interest naturally congregates.

One very hopeful experiment has been made in the Panjâb. Here there are in the great "Doâbs" or tracts between two rivers—in the central parts equally removed from the moistening influence of either river—great stretches of alluvial land fertile enough if artificially irrigated, but which can only be irrigated by expensive State-made canal works. In some cases Government has been able to provide the water, laying out (with reference to the straight canal cuts and cross channels) a number of rectangular blocks suitable to form holdings, a number of which will aggregate into an (artificial) "village." Here the (originally waste) land belongs, without any question, to the State; and so (by law) does the water; hence it is possible that all settlers, who can be tempted away from the "congested" districts, can be located as Government tenants, at a very moderate rent and revenue rate, and *without any power of alienation.* This plan, though recent, has now been in working for some time. But we have not heard much of its results; but, as far as I know, they have been very satisfactory. It is a great pity that this and similar matters concerning the economic welfare of the peasantry are not thought more worthy of occasional notice by local "correspondents." The Panjâb scheme has been worked on a considerable scale. For example, the Doâb near the Chinâb River contains many hundred thousand cultivable acres laid out in this way; and there are other centres. The Panjâb Government has to deal with (on the whole) varied and superior agricultural races, a large proportion of whom cultivate their own lands.

In existing villages, the Panjâb law does not encourage the dissolution of the bond of joint responsibility; and a village cannot become separated completely into independent parts, except when a "Settlement" (p. 28) is in progress, and then under special conditions. In the N.W. Provinces, a much larger proportion of the village owners employ tenants, and look to rental rather than to cultivating profits. Here there is hardly any restriction on complete severance (including the revenue responsibility) so long as all concerned agree in asking for it. And the plan is commonly adopted of allowing separate landholders in the villages to pay their own share of the revenue and rates direct into the local treasury.[1] The tendency of the N.W.P. villages is certainly towards their becoming completely *raiyatwâri*, though the title to the holding is that of complete proprietary right. And in all cases where the owner is of a

[1] Ordinarily they pay to the *lambardâr* or representative head of the village, or of the section (*patti*) to which they belong, the representative being personally responsible for the total being paid in. Complaints became frequent that the payments made to this person were misapplied, on one pretext or another; hence the rule that permission to pay direct might be given. But this tends powerfully to break up the idea of a "community."

non-agricultural caste, originally or by purchase, we shall have a series of small properties, often held by non-resident owners, and worked by tenants, some having "occupancy" rights, and other privileges under the Tenant Law,[1] some being tenants at will paying what is already, virtually, a competition rent. Such properties will probably tend gradually to reaccumulate in the hands of a few owners, who will buy up first one plot and then another, and have estates scattered in plots through half-a-dozen villages or more; but the "village" will be only a geographical or survey unit; it will hardly have any meaning, except as a monument of some forgotten unity, which may be once more gilded by the halo of theories.

[1] It would be beyond my scope to explain the nature of the Tenant Law, which, as may be supposed, is chiefly needed in the Northern Provinces where there are landlords, or joint-villages employing tenants, and where these tenants are often the remains of older settlers whose rights have been overborne, but too long ago to make it possible to do more than recognise certain privileges attaching to long possession. There is a general account of the Tenancy Law in my little book called "A Short Account of the Land Administration of British India" (Clarendon Press, 1894), pp. 133-144.

APPENDIX I

It has been stated (p, 109) that the belief in an original "communal" form of village in peninsular India was largely due to the conservation of some forms of joint village, which (without asking anything in detail as to their date or other features), were at once *assumed* to be ancient, and to represent relics of an early universal common ownership. I therefore briefly sketch the different cases where such survivals occur.

I. In Bombay we find (*a*) in the Gujarât districts a limited number of actually existing joint villages—in strong contrast with the "severalty" villages all round. In the Dakhan districts there are only traces of a (more ancient) *mirâsi* tenure prevailing from former times down to the days of the Mahrâthas. II. In Madras, especially in the Chingleput district and the immediate vicinity, we have (fast disappearing) traces of a privileged co-sharing tenure of villages, also called by the Moslems *mirâsi*, and by the indigenous people *kâniâtsi*.

I. (*a*) In some of the Gujarât districts a limited number of villages (*narwâdâri* and *bhâgdâri*) are known to be comparatively modern, though a precise date is not assignable. In both cases they represent the growth of certain dominant families over the village. In the Broach district these are Bohra [1] families, often descended from one ancestor. In the Kaira district villages the families are of the Kunbi caste, and here apparently (in some cases) several families had originally joined together for the purpose of restoring cultivation or taking the revenue responsibility. In time, the families multiplying in num-

[1] The Bohra are a caste partly of traders, partly of agriculturists. The Kunbi are the well-known cultivating caste of Western India. The total number of these villages does not exceed 347 ("L. S. B. I.," Vol. III., p. 260). The largest number is in the Broach district, much fewer in Kaira, and about a dozen in Sûrat.

bers, divided their interests and responsibilities in suitable shares. But (as usual) they kept together as jointly liable bodies, without which they would have soon lost their privileged position. As it was, these dominant bodies came to constitute *the* community—the joint proprietors of the whole village. The Bohras adopted the plan of dividing into fractional shares, according to the "ancestral" system, following the table of descent—each share of the holding corresponds to a similar fraction of the revenue liability.[1] The Kunbis (being probably associate groups of different families) contracted for a lump sum of revenue on the whole village, and proceeded to divide it and the cultivation—not by (ancestral) fractional shares—but by arranging groups of cultivation (including portions of each kind of soil), and making out a *narwâ* or distribution scheme, which apportioned the revenue responsibility over the holdings of the different sections or family groups.

(*b*) The more interesting ancient *mirâsi* traces in many Dakhan villages are fully discussed in a paper contributed by me to the Royal Asiatic Society's Journal in 1897.[2] It was long ago noticed that in these villages certain lands were said to be *mirâsi*, and had once constituted *shares* in a property which, in fact, included the whole village. In some cases the complete list of shares could still be traced, and they were all known by Hindu-Aryan names, and the holders were superior in rank and dignity. Looking back at the known early history of Western India, I think there can be no doubt that these were the shares in villages which had become dominated by families of some rank, perhaps connected with the Yâdava kingdom of Dêvagirî, or with the Châlukya or the Râshtrakûta clans, all well known to history and to our epigraphists. These, being of military, not agricultural caste, perished in the wars that (as a matter of fact) overthrew the Yâdava and Châlukya kingdoms in the Middle Ages. The names and *locale* of the shares (*bhâg*) remained, owing to the tenacity of tradition which is so notorious throughout the East ; and as the *mirâs* tenure was an advantageous one, it was found possible (for a long time) to continue

[1] For details and examples, see "Ind. Vill. Comm.," p. 386 ff.

[2] Vol. for 1897, April, p. 239. See also my "Ind. Vill. Comm.," p. 380 ff.

the privilege, and fill the vacant holdings by the revenue authorities granting (or even selling) the *mirâs* title. Here, then, we have only the "manorial" growth of dominant, co-sharing families over the villages. But in this case the families shared the misfortunes of their race and disappeared; while in other parts of India the joint families persisted, multiplied, and furnished quite numerous "communities," dominating the villages, and introducing their own co-sharing constitution.

II. The vestiges of *mirâsi* tenure in Madras are of a different order.[1] Tradition in this case—as accepted by all the best authorities—is supported by the caste and other features of the villages, which were still plainly in evidence at the end of the eighteenth century. They were chiefly mediæval villages established by a succession of immigrants of a peculiar agricultural race (Vellâlan) from North Kânara and elsewhere, who were with difficulty induced to settle by the promise of exceptional privileges, and a permanent interest in the villages they established. The success of this special colonising enterprise, after many failures, is referred to the efforts of one of the later Chôlâ kings who ruled in the eleventh century A.D. The case was altogether exceptional; and the families appear to have found a close co-operation necessary, both to insure a victory over the difficulties of the enterprise, and also to secure among themselves the due sharing of the privileged tenure, with its partial exemption from taxation. We have fair evidence of their mode of allotting the lands each year for cultivation, and of sharing the profits. In some cases they actually divided the shares on the ground permanently.[2]

In all these cases we have varieties of ways in which a special privilege, a grant, or even the usurpation, of families of superior ability or rank, results in producing a joint body of proprietors.

[1] These are the traces discussed in the volume entitled "Mirâsi Papers," Madras, 1862, to which Sir H. S. Maine once alludes (see p. 36).

[2] The details are given in "Ind. Vill. Comm.," p. 362 ff. Of course colonist parties have been found in other parts of India, most commonly on a smaller scale, and with no particular difficulties to contend with, so that exceptional advantages are not expected or granted. In the S.E. Panjâb many (individual) villages were founded by colonist bodies, who hav fallen into the joint village class because they readily accepted a joint liability for revenue (pp. 94-5).

In some cases it is over existing severalty villages; in others, the dominant groups (with the same sense of superiority) have occupied newly established villages, so that there were no former landholders to become vassals, but only such slaves, tenants, and helpers as the superior settlers themselves introduced and located. But the whole circumstances in each case clearly negative the idea that in such traces we have a primitive and general institution. The *raiyatwâri* was the general form, the *mirâsi* right a special and privileged growth in and over it, and it certainly had nothing of a communistic character. In so brief a note I have not attempted to allude to every instance of an alleged *mirâsi* interest in Madras; but an examination of any village to which the term *mirâsi* can properly be applied, in districts other than Chingleput, will *always* show that it is a case of some grant or dominant right acquired.

Printed by Cowan & Co., Limited, Perth.